A Great Ca
for Beauty

The Tiffany Glass Collection at the Haworth Art Gallery, Accrington

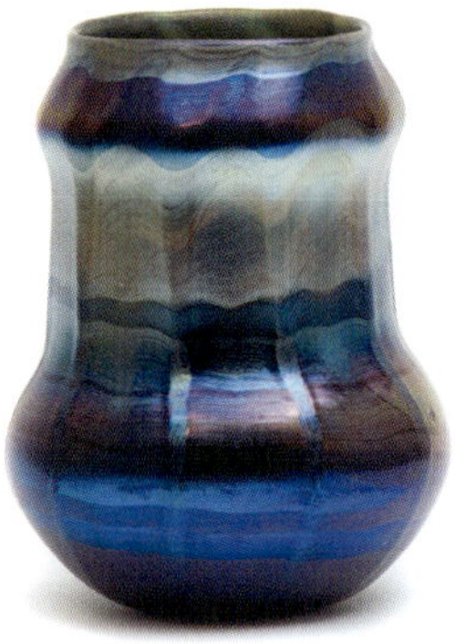

Commissioned by Hyndburn Borough Council with the aid of a Bequest from the late Stephen Moore of Altham

Written by Jennifer A Rennie

This publication marks the 120th anniversary of Joseph Briggs's voyage from Liverpool to seek his fortune in America. The journey resulted, some 40 years later, in the Haworth's extraordinary Tiffany glass collection making the voyage back.

Blue Vase (above and detail, left), cat. no. 7 **Peacock Vase** (front cover, detail), cat. no. 2

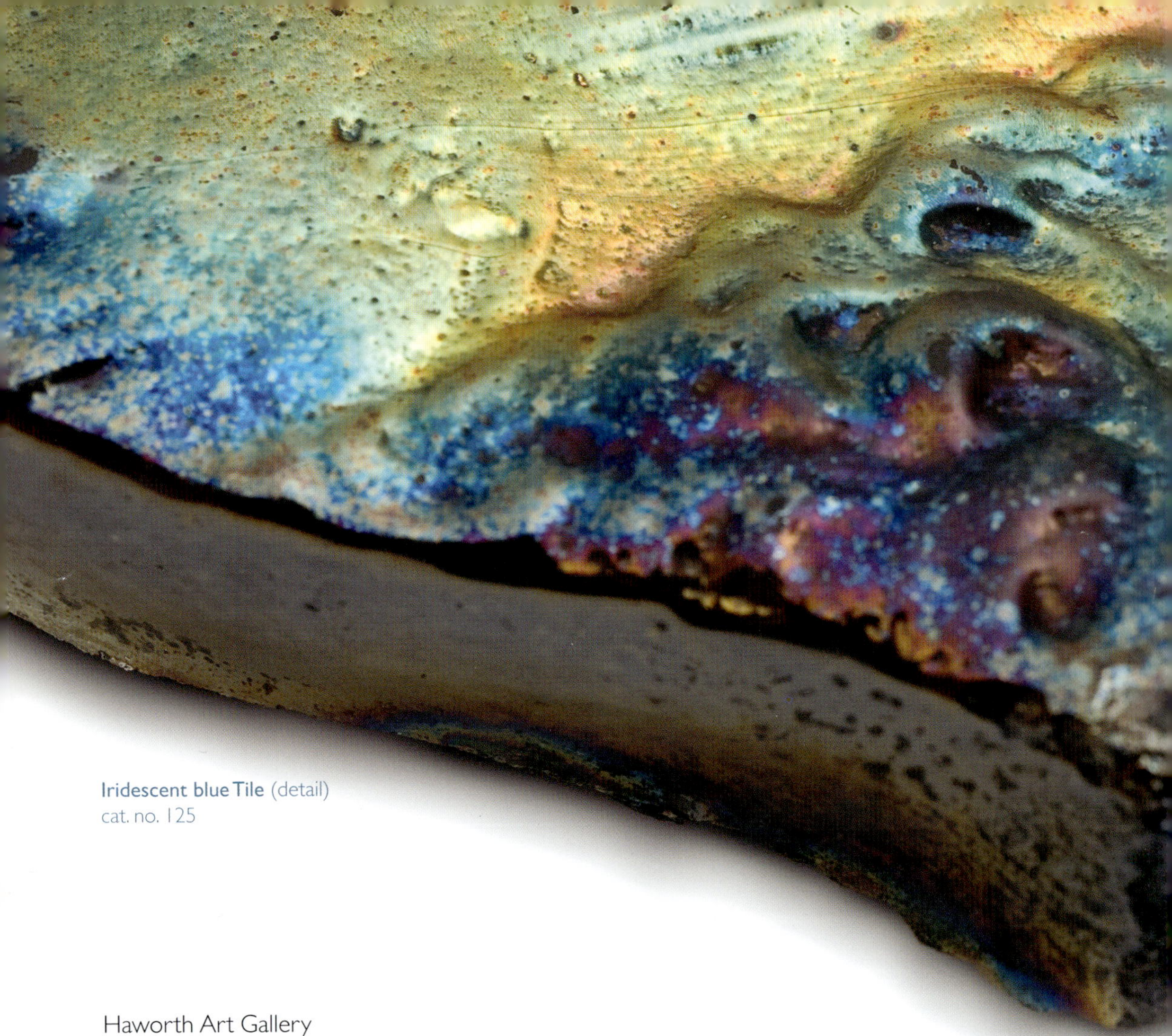

Iridescent blue Tile (detail)
cat. no. 125

Haworth Art Gallery
Manchester Road
Accrington
Lancashire
BB5 2JS
Tel 01254 233782

www.hyndburnbc.gov.uk/hag

ISBN: 978-0-9571876-0-3
Catalogue in publication data available.
Published by Hyndburn Borough Council, 2012.

HYNDBURN
The place to be
an excellent council

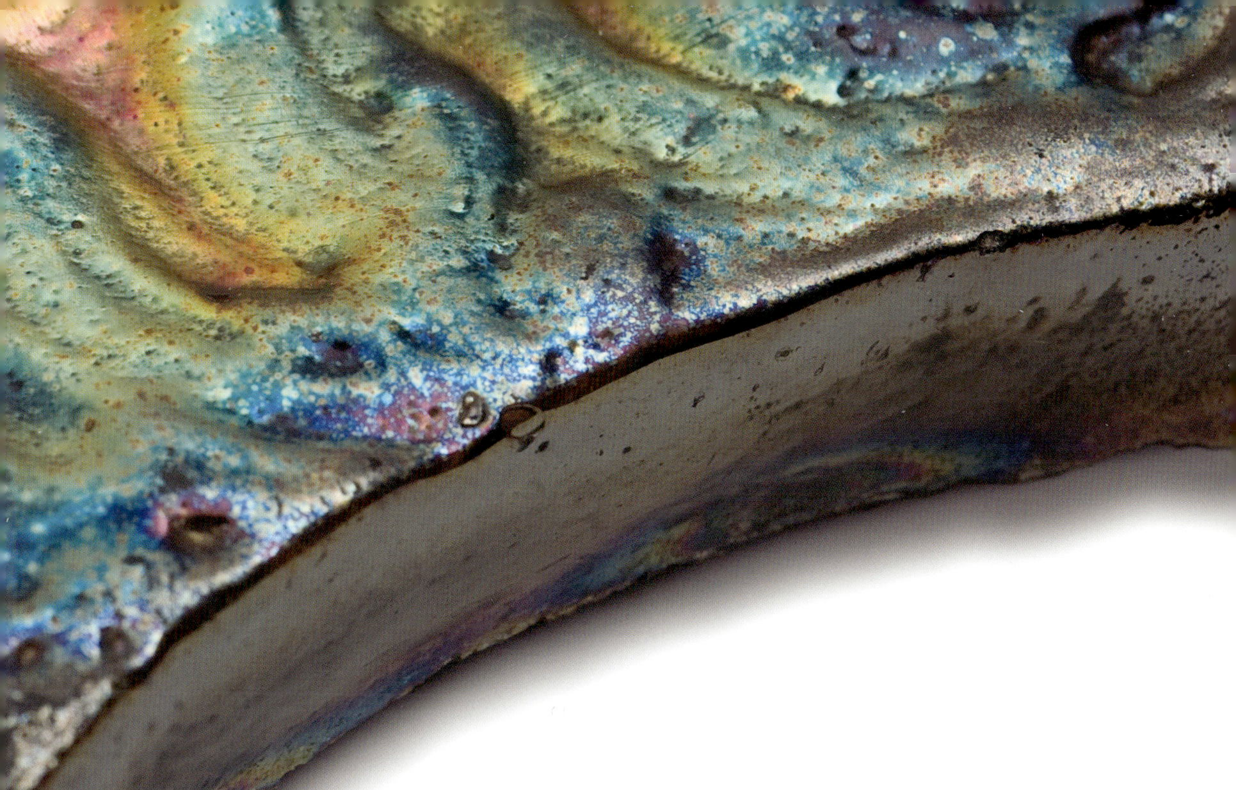

Contents

Foreword by Eric Knowles 5

Accrington-New York-Accrington 7

Life of Joseph Briggs 13

Louis Comfort Tiffany: Striving to fix Beauty 15

Life of Louis Comfort Tiffany 21

Layering Colours: Tiffany *Favrile* Vases 23

Catalogue of the Haworth Art Gallery's Tiffany Glass Collection 37

Acknowledgements and Further Reading 60

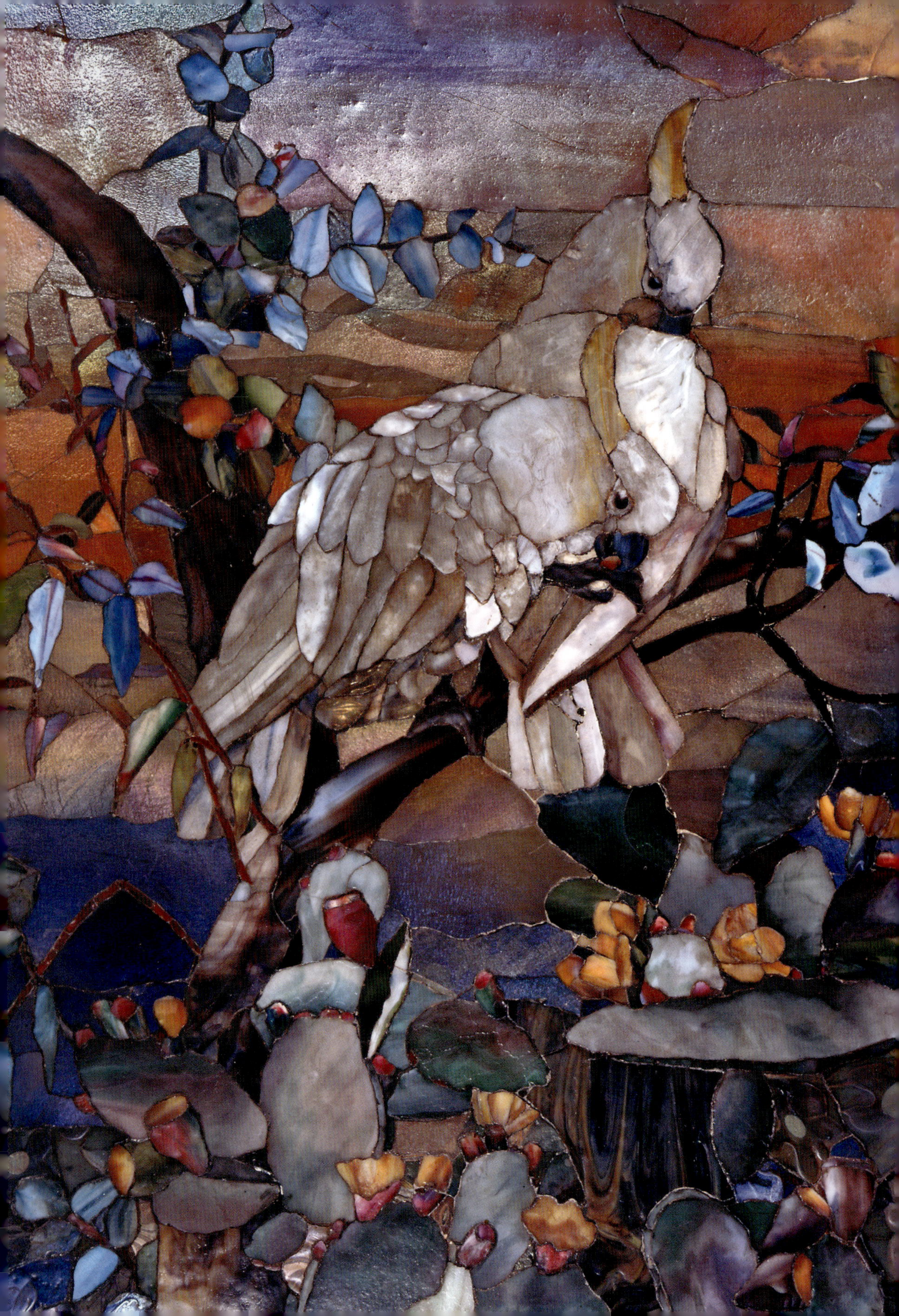

The Haworth Art Gallery
by Eric Knowles

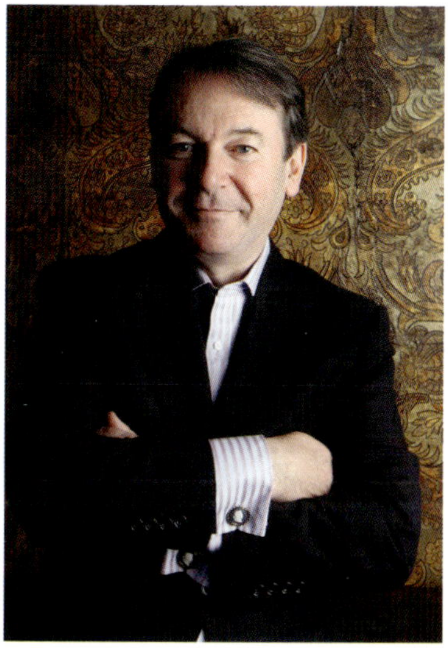

It was many years ago that I came to realise that the fates had been exceptionally kind by having ensured that I was born and raised in that part of North East Lancashire dominated by Pendle Hill. It was here that as a boy I soon became aware that I was living in a region surrounded by historical sites on a grand scale, with its fair share of castles, abbeys, a Roman fort and no shortage of superb museums - not forgetting the infamous Pendle Witches.

Fast forward to 1979, by which time I was running the all new *Art Nouveau* and *Art Deco* department at Bonhams auction house in London, and enter the Haworth Art Gallery. This was the year that I was invited to provide an inventory of the Gallery's contents. The 'Haworth' could justifiably claim to have on permanent display what is unquestionably the finest public collection of Tiffany glass outside the USA. This had all come about by the generosity of a certain Joseph Briggs - a local lad made good who had left for New York in 1891 and eventually gained employ with Louis Comfort Tiffany. Having become, with the passage of time, a senior figure in the company, he bequeathed his important Tiffany glass collection to the Borough of Accrington in the early 1930s.

Today it is beautifully displayed in cabinets captioned with concise information that explains the ethos, influences and manufacturing techniques involved, all of which has proved popular with the Gallery's many visitors - both young and old. But there is so much more to this art gallery and museum, such as its highly important collection of watercolours and oil paintings not to mention the fine ceramics, glass and silver. The dedicated curatorial team continually organises 'must see' exhibitions and ensure that this is very much a people's museum devoid of any hint of elitism.

As a veteran of BBC's *Antiques Roadshow* it has always been my mission to recognise and tell the nation about newly discovered gems. The good folk of Accrington are indeed fortunate to have such a jewel in the 'Haworth' but for goodness sake don't take my word for it - just go and see for yourself!

Mosaic Panel with
Sulphur-Crested
Cockatoos
cat. no. 77

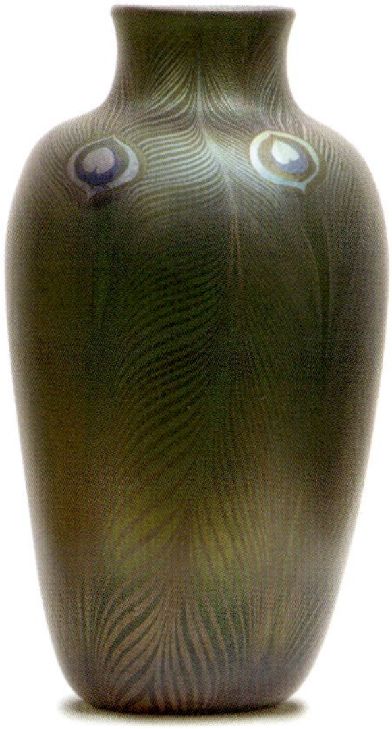

Peacock Vase
cat. no. 2

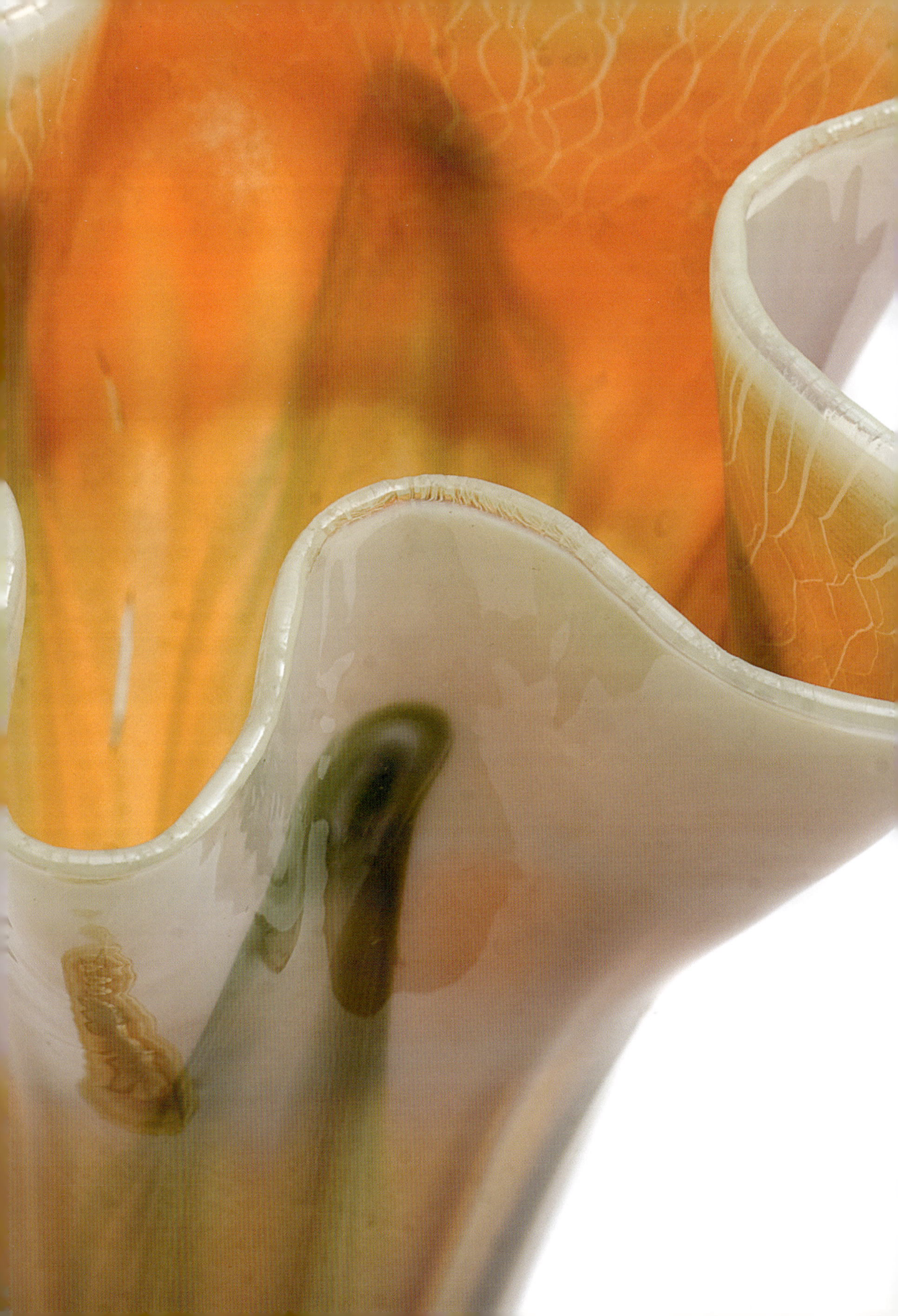

Accrington-New York-Accrington

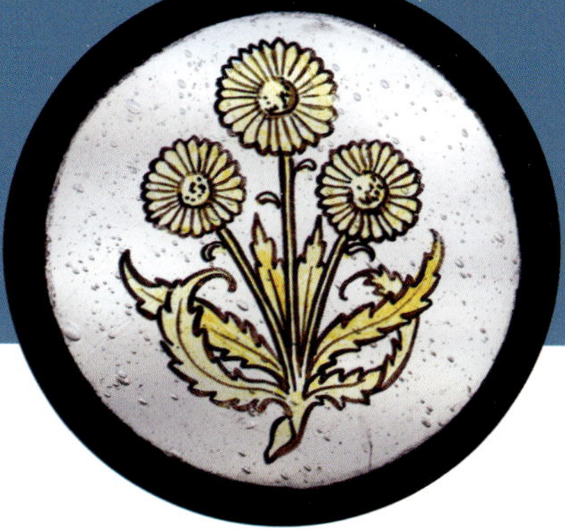

The Haworth Art Gallery is in Accrington, a town in East Lancashire in the heart of England's former cotton manufacturing area. An Edwardian Tudor Mansion in the Arts and Crafts style[1], it is home to a rare and fabulous collection of over 140 examples of the work of Louis Comfort Tiffany (1848-1933), the foremost exponent of *Art Nouveau* in the United States of America. *Art Nouveau,* meaning 'New Art,' was an international movement in the decorative arts and architecture which used the structures, colours and forms of the natural world in fundamentally new ways. It swept Europe and America in the first decade of the 20th century.

Favrile Glass

Tiffany's chosen medium for the creation of his *Art Nouveau* masterpieces was his *Favrile,* meaning 'hand-made', glass. Tiffany *Favrile* glass-makers decorated their glass while forming it with the blow-pipe, creating unique pieces in radical new shapes with stunning colour effects. Tiffany's various organisations made every type of decorative glass for public and private American interiors. From architectural schemes in glass mosaics and stained-glass windows to glass lampshades, vases and tableware, Tiffany's products enabled him to transform interiors with the infinite variety of colour and form he found so inspiring in nature.

The Haworth's glass collection was sent from New York in 1932 and 1933 by Accrington-born Joseph Briggs (1873-1938) and is the largest public collection of Tiffany's work on permanent display in Europe. Briggs had worked for Tiffany for over 40 years and whether it was his personal collection or a selection of what remained when the furnaces and studios finally closed, it forms an extraordinary group, containing examples of almost every type of *Favrile* glass that Tiffany made. For anyone wishing to see a substantial display of Tiffany glass outside America, a visit to the Haworth's four galleries is a must, while the building itself offers a direct though restrained Arts and Crafts equivalent to the rich, flamboyant colour and form associated with the best of Tiffany glass.

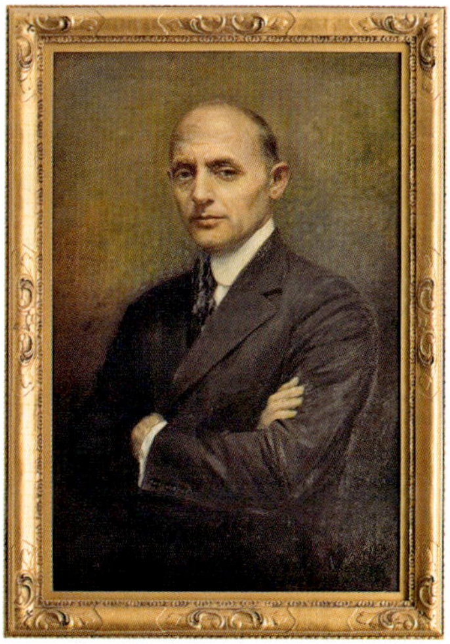

Arts and Crafts motif: Daisy flowers with Dandelion leaves. (top), staircase window, Haworth Art Gallery (not Tiffany)

Flower Form Vase (detail) cat. no. 4

Portrait of Joseph Briggs, 1924. O. Segall. Haworth Art Gallery Collection

From New York by Sea

Records are scant regarding the arrival in Accrington of the three crates of *Art Nouveau* glass from New York. The Parks and Cemeteries Committee recorded the gift of two cases of Tiffany vases on 14 July 1932 and of 'a number of vases and tiles' on 16 March 1933. A further minute of 17 August 1933 records the receipt of 'gifts from Mr. Joseph Briggs, 46 West Twenty-third Street, New York.'[2] Typed slips in the day-book of the Town's former Museum in Oak Hill Park recorded more details of the 1933 deposits.[3] Forty-two pieces of the glass were soon put on display in Room 8 of the Museum, recorded as the gift of 'Joseph Briggs, Esq, Art Director and Assistant Manager of the Tiffany Studios Corporation of New York', though Museum labels acknowledge the donor as the Briggs Family of Milnshaw Lane.[4] Briggs's family are known to have visited him in New York and were certainly involved with the arrangements for the gift.[5]

James Priestley Aspden remembered a crate of Tiffany glass being delivered to Accrington Town Hall by two brothers, members of Briggs's family.[6] The curator of the Museum, Mr Albert Hanson, was summoned to give his opinion and he agreed the identification.

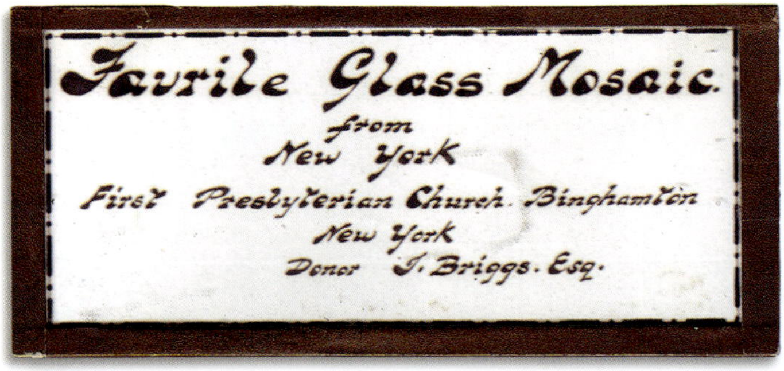

Original Oak Hill Park Museum labels for the Tiffany glass collection. (Haworth Tiffany Archive)

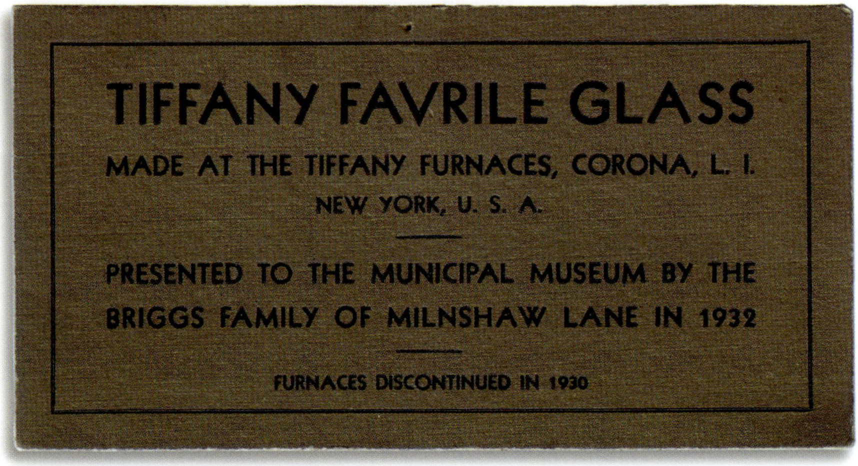

In newspaper reports he praised the exquisite beauty of the glass and pointed out that Accrington's Museum was now joining "principal museums in Berlin and Paris" in displaying Tiffany's award-winning glass.[7] No doubt Hanson made the selection for the Oak Hill Park display which was on show until the Museum closed at the outbreak of World War II in September 1939. The display was eventually dismantled and moved to the Haworth's basement for safe-keeping, along with the remainder of the Tiffany collection which had been stored at the Town Hall.

Tiffany Glass at the Haworth

Excitement at the fact of such a collection being given to the town was slow to build. Older visitors to the Haworth recall seeing Tiffany glass vases full of wild flowers on window-sills and the story of Accrington's glamorous collection of Tiffany glass was recorded only in a routine way in the *Municipal Journal* in 1961.[8] Hubert Rigg, appointed curator at the Haworth in 1962, arranged the first secure cased display of about 60 vases which remained until the North West Museum Service (NWMS) unveiled a more sophisticated display in 1977. The collection was illuminated in cases around the edge of a darkened ground-floor room but had to be dismantled when dry rot was discovered in the walls. A second redisplay, opened in 1991 and also funded by NWMS, allowed the Briggs Gift to be seen in its entirety for the first time. Since then, the display has been expanded to four rooms, enabling more space and natural light to be given to the collection, additional information to be included and permitting far more visitors to enjoy the Tiffany pieces at any one time.[9]

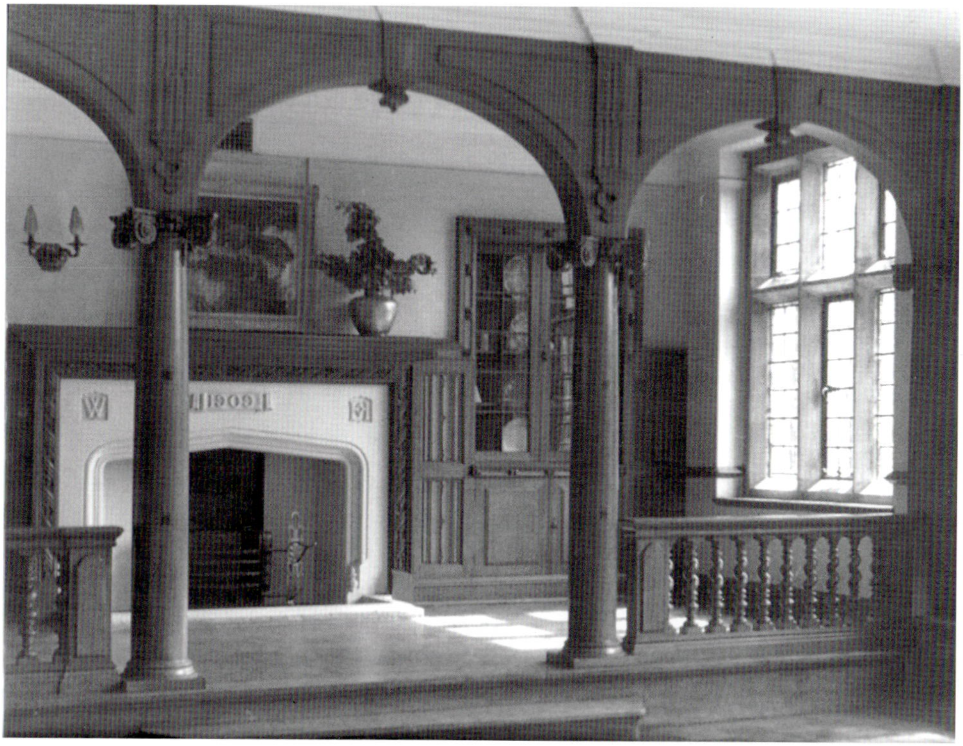

A Tiffany vase, cat. no. 32, in the Haworth's music room, holding flowers. (Haworth Tiffany Archive)

Tiffany and Briggs

The story of the relationship between the illustrious maker of some of the most complex and beautiful decorative glass in the world and a pattern designer from an East Lancashire cotton town is an intriguing one. Books about Tiffany make only fleeting reference to Briggs, yet he was important enough to be one of only two people appointed by Tiffany to take over the running of the company on his retirement in 1918.[10]

Briggs began working for Tiffany due to two extraordinary flukes of timing. In 1891 Briggs, aged 17 years, arranged an extended leave from his apprenticeship and set off to seek his fortune in America, eventually settling in New York. At this point, Tiffany was expanding his glass-making activities and Briggs applied for one of the jobs Tiffany was advertising. After an unsuccessful interview, Briggs found himself outside Tiffany Studios in the rain where he bumped into a very well-dressed man. Briggs offered him the use of his umbrella and a conversation led to the man, who turned out to be Tiffany himself, suggesting he try again. He asked Briggs to make a design for a stained-glass window and the result, showing *St Peter at the Gates of Heaven holding the Keys,* began a working relationship which would last until Tiffany's death in 1933.[11] Maybe Tiffany saw echoes of himself as a young man when he gave Briggs this life-changing opportunity. He may have sensed how much they had in common despite their different backgrounds. Both had refused to go along with their fathers' plans for their sons' careers. Furthermore, both had travelled long distances to follow their dreams, Briggs to America, Tiffany to Europe.

Sampler for the Christ Episcopal Church, Brooklyn, New York (detail), cat. no. 80

Working at Tiffany Studios as an errand boy and general handyman, Briggs used any spare time to teach himself how to cut glass squares and create mosaic pictures. Tiffany noticed Briggs's determination to better himself and had him trained in the stained-glass window and mosaics shops. It was not long before Briggs was employed as chief assistant to Clara Driscoll, soon to become a highly-paid designer of Tiffany lamps.[12]

Tiffany's opinion of Briggs grew to the extent that when Tiffany inherited the increased workload of his father's business in 1902[13], Briggs became foreman manager of the mosaics shop which produced all Tiffany Studios' architectural mosaics schemes. He also worked on the company's representation at World Fairs, making the *Sulphur - Crested Cockatoos mosaic* around 1908 to demonstrate the rare beauty and great variety of Tiffany's *Favrile* glass.

St George and the Dragon
cat. no. 144

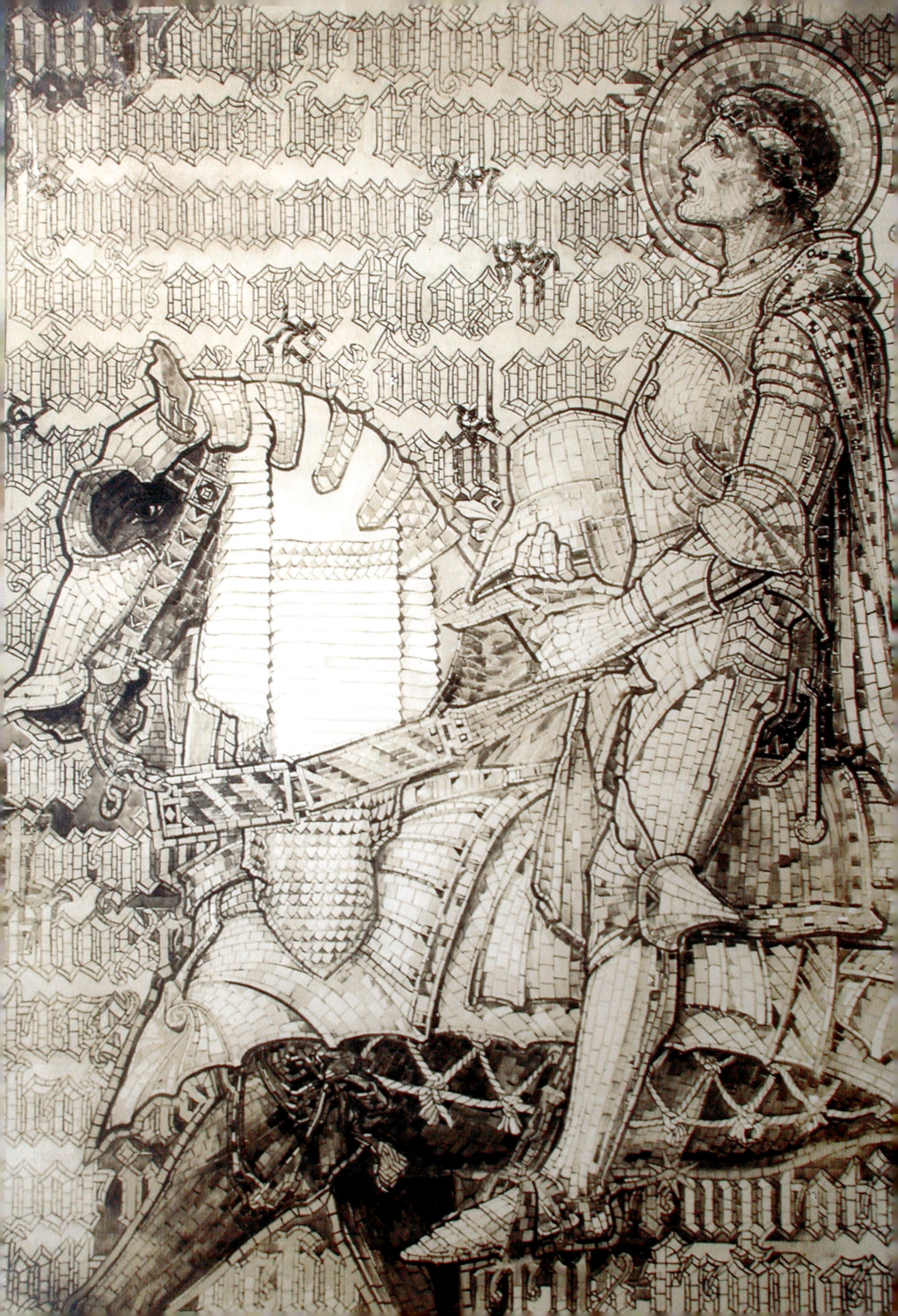

In 1912 Briggs moved to a large purpose-built house in Wood Ridge, New Jersey. As well as being home to Briggs's growing family, the house contained stunning examples of Tiffany glass and several floral Tiffany windows. It was a sort of 'show home,' used to demonstrate how Tiffany products enhanced the quality of everyday life.[14] This arrangement was only possible because Briggs was wholly dedicated to the success of the company and underlines why he was known as Tiffany's 'Right-hand man.'

Briggs's work with Tiffany continued to focus on architectural mosaics and the Haworth's mosaic samplers and drawings for the Philadelphia Mint, the St Louis Cathedral Lady Chapel and Christ Church, Brooklyn, relate directly to him. Briggs is also known to have worked alongside Tiffany in the selection and firing of thousands of glass tesserae for the fabulous *Dream Garden Mosaic* at the Curtis Publishing Company in Philadelphia in 1915-16.[15]

After Tiffany's retirement in 1919, Briggs's importance became even more evident. As a trustee of the LC Tiffany Foundation and head of Tiffany Studios, he was increasingly involved in the day-to-day financial management of Tiffany's various enterprises. Briggs, having worked with Tiffany for many years, was known to him for his abilities as a designer, manager and promoter. He was therefore trusted to manage and eventually oversee the winding-down of Tiffany's various organisations and finally became Tiffany's chief executor.[16] In 1924, on the closing of Tiffany Furnaces, the entire stock of Tiffany Favrile glass was given to Briggs and sold over several years, but being by now considered old-fashioned, even worthless, it achieved only paltry sums. After Tiffany's death, and at his express wish, Briggs took over as Art Director of the Louis C Tiffany Studios Corporation, set up in 1932, a position he held until his own death in 1938.

---

1 The Arts and Crafts movement advocated 'Truth to materials' and traditional craftsmanship inspired by medieval or folk arts.

2 Accrington Borough Council Minutes Books, 1932 and 1933. Accrington Local Studies Library.

3 Photocopies of typed entries for 10 March and 10 July 1933, Oak Hill Park Museum day book. The second consignment consisted of '18 Tiffany *Favril* Vases' and '50 Glass Decorative Tiles'. The third of '7 Mosaic panels, 10 Sketch prints, 14 Vases, 3 Enamel placques, 1 Silver Tray'. Present whereabouts unknown.

4 *Guide to Oak Hill Park Museum,* 1933. Accrington Local Studies Library.

5 Examples of Tiffany glass were sold through Christie's salerooms in the early 1980s by members of the Briggs family and a Lava vase which was brought to BBC television's *Antiques Road Show* at Hyndburn Sports Centre in March 1995 is likely to have belonged to them originally.

6 Account given to Jennifer Rennie by Richard Haworth Aspden, 3 November 2005. Mr Aspden was Accrington's Director of Development and Works from September 1970 to August 1980. His brother, James Priestley Aspden, was articled clerk to the Town Clerk WH Warhurst from October 1933 to May 1947.

7 *Accrington Observer and Times,* 15 Oct 1932 and 11 Oct 1933.

8 *Accrington's Favrile Glass* by J Dove in *The Municipal Journal,* 5 May 1961.

9 Redisplay by Redman Design, funded by the Heritage Lottery Fund, Hyndburn Borough Council and the anonymous bequest of a Baxenden couple, 2001/2.

10 A Douglas Nash (1885-1940) took over Tiffany Furnaces as Briggs took over Tiffany Studios.

11 The story of this chance meeting was told by Joseph Ashworth Briggs II on his visit to the Haworth in 1992.

12 Tiffany's readiness to employ women led to unrest and a strike threat in 1903. See *A New Light on Tiffany - Clara Driscoll and the Tiffany Girls* by Eidelberg, Grey and Hoffer, New York, 2007, for information on the employment of women in America at this time.

13 Tiffany's father was Charles Louis Tiffany (1812-1902), founder of Tiffany & Co, Silversmiths and Jewellers.

14 A Tiffany stained-glass window with clematis and a pair of side windows from Briggs's house were sold at Sotheby's, New York, in December 1999.

15 It took Tiffany Studios a year to make the 24 panels of this mosaic, after the specially-commissioned painting by Maxfield Parrish (1870-1966). The panels were exhibited for a month before being transported to Philadelphia, where they took a further 6 months to install. See *The Mosaics of Louis Comfort Tiffany* by Edith Crouch, pp. 265-271.

16 In the last years of his life, Tiffany remained close to three people: Stanley Lothrop, Director of the Tiffany Foundation at Laurelton Hall, Sarah Hanley, the Irish nurse who cared for him up until his death and Joseph Briggs.

Life of Joseph Briggs

1873	Born on 11 December at 3, Milnshaw Lane, Accrington, one of seven children; his father was a foreman engraver at Steiner's calico printing works in Church, near Accrington.
1887	Began apprenticeship with his father as a calico engraver.
1891	21 September, left Liverpool on the *SS Servia,* bound for New York.
1891-93/4	Unknown occupation, travelled the USA.
1893/4	Taken on by Louis Comfort Tiffany at the Tiffany Glass and Decorating Company.
1896	Made first mosaic, using stained-glass window off-cuts. Became Clara Driscoll's chief assistant around this time.
1898	Married Elizabeth Jenkins of Virginia.
1899	Birth of son Joseph Ashworth, first of six children.
1900/1	Six-month visit to England, bringing his wife and children.
1901	1 July, death of Joseph Ashworth, in Manhattan.
1902	Promoted to foreman manager of the mosaics shop at Tiffany Studios.
1906	Became an American citizen.
1912	Began a weekly commute from his New Jersey home to Tiffany Studios in Manhattan.
1918	Appointed Managing Director of Tiffany Studios and Trustee of the LC Tiffany Foundation.
1932	Filed for bankruptcy of Tiffany Studios and sent the first of three cases of Tiffany glass to Accrington.
1933	On the death of Tiffany, Briggs disposed of all assets of Tiffany Studios and sent two more cases of Tiffany glass to Accrington.
1938	30 March, died in a New York hospital, aged 64 years.

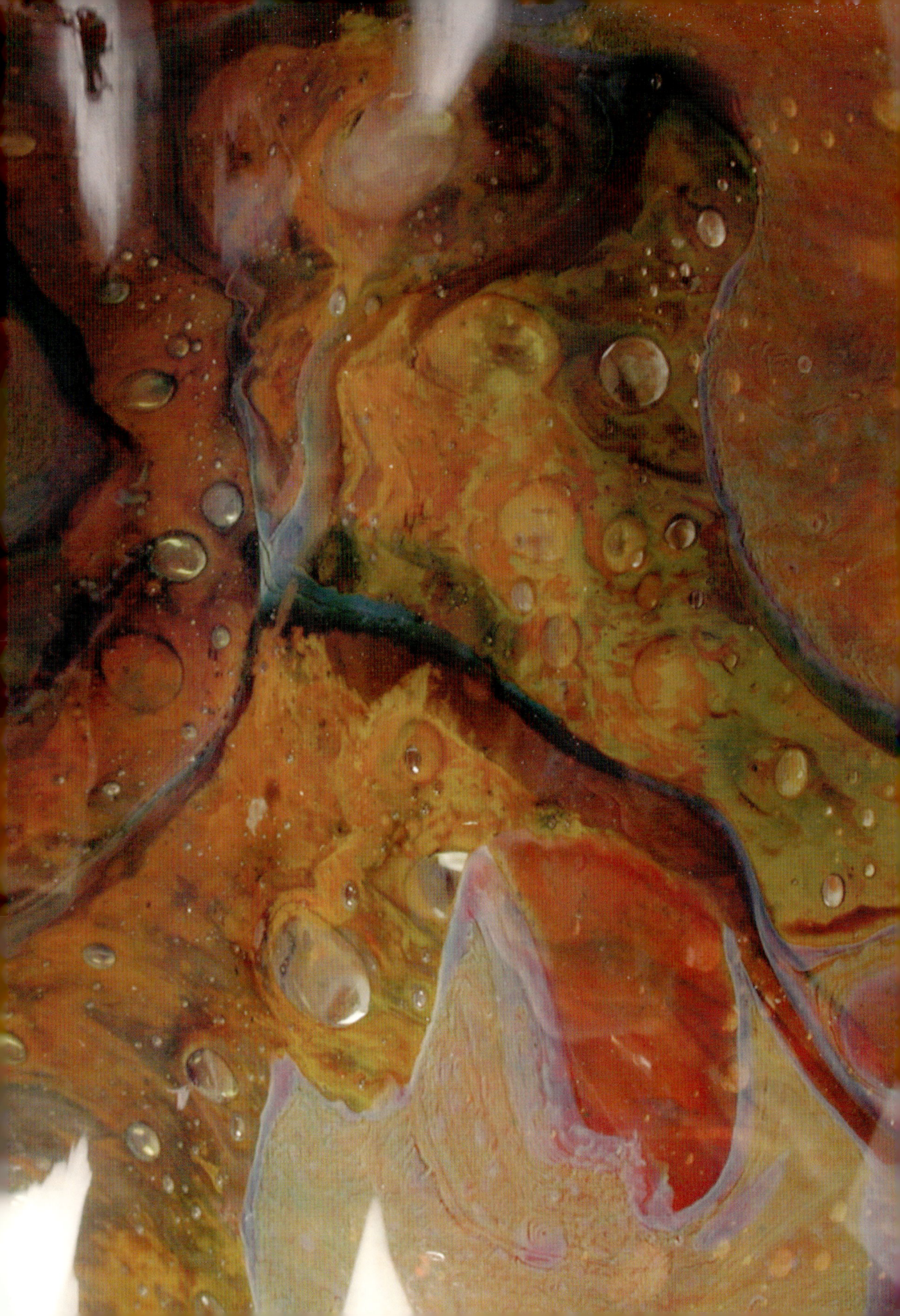

Louis Comfort Tiffany: Striving to Fix Beauty

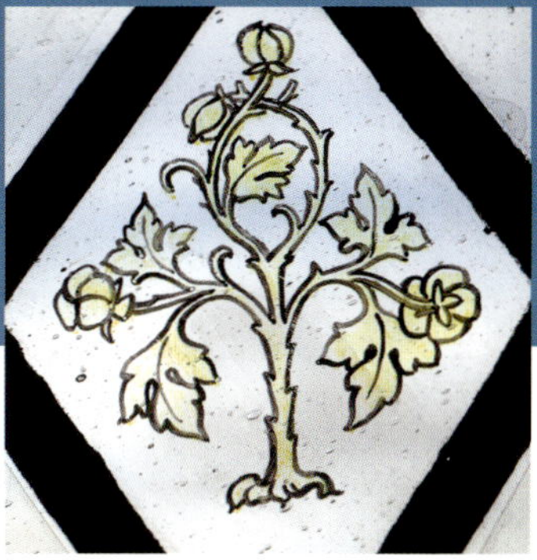

"I have always striven to fix beauty in wood or stone or glass or pottery, in oil or water color..."

Tiffany's statement about his life's work was made on the occasion of his 68th Birthday in 1916.[1] The following year he gave an impassioned description of how, after a visit to North Africa as a young man, he had realised that colour was to be his chief tool for 'fixing beauty.' The paintings Tiffany produced during this eight-month trip to Europe and Africa were exhibited to great acclaim in New York in the 1870s but Tiffany was moving away from landscape paintings and towards the decorative arts. He was experimenting with glass at Thill's glass works in Brooklyn and teaching and exhibiting with the Society of Decorative Arts. In 1878, inspired by the colours and cultures of the East, he transformed the interior and furnishings of his own home and studio. The popularity of these renovations led to his launching no fewer than three interior design companies: *Tiffany and Wheeler* in 1879 and *LC Tiffany and Company, Furniture* and *Tiffany and de Forest, Decorators* in 1880.

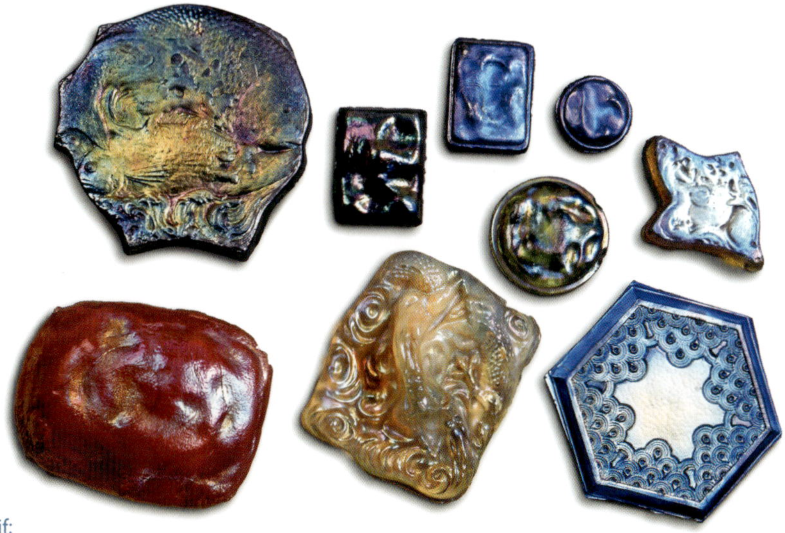

Arts and Crafts motif: Rose Bush (top), staircase window, Haworth Art Gallery (not Tiffany)

Paperweight Vase (detail) cat. no. 60

Selection of tiles and jewels loaned to the Hamburg Tiffany exhibition, 1999. Tiffany used tiles and jewels for experiments in the 1870s with colour in glass.

American Interiors

The name Louis Comfort Tiffany conjures up images of elegant, beautiful and lavish interiors in the public and private buildings of late 19th century America. In his interior designs, Tiffany mixed the vibrant colours of the natural world, an appreciation of world cultures and the art of the past, while incorporating modern inventions like central heating and electric lighting.[2] Amongst his early commissions were author Mark Twain's house in Hartford, Connecticut and the Library and Veterans' rooms in the Seventh Regiment Armory building in New York, both of which can be visited today.[3]

Tiffany was at the forefront of interior design and decorative arts in America for three decades. He produced textiles, wallpapers, stained-glass windows for both secular and religious buildings, memorials, mosaic walls, floors and ceilings, light fittings, vases, furniture, tableware, desk-ware, pottery, enamels and jewellery. But it was after he had visited mosques lit by glass lamps in North Africa and churches illuminated by stained-glass windows in France, that he realised that glass was an under-exploited vehicle for creating colour and atmosphere in interiors.

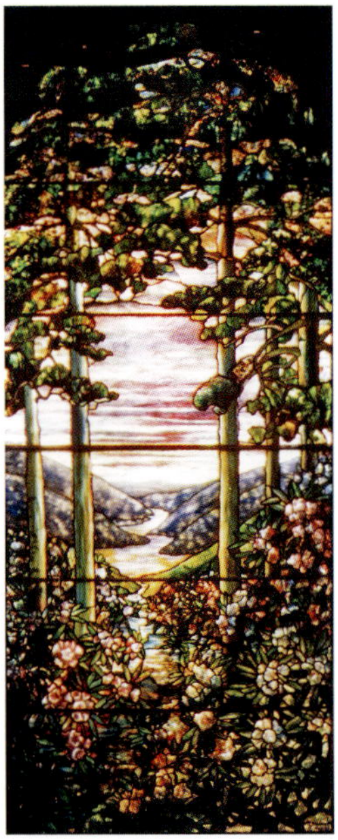

Stained glass window by Tiffany Studios in Andrew Carnegie House, Dunfermline. (Photograph courtesy of the Carnegie Dunfimline Trust)

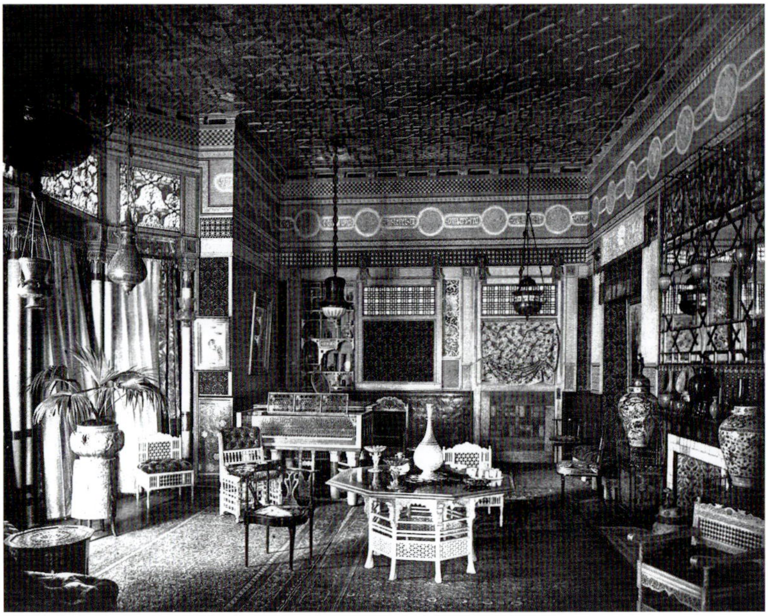

'Mr George Kemp's Salon', *Artistic Houses, Interior Views of the Most Beautiful and Celebrated Homes in the United States,* New York, D. Appleton and Co., 1883, vol. 1, part 1, no. 21. (Photograph courtesy of the Smithsonian Institution Libraries, Washington, DC)

Tiffany eventually made many hundreds of stained-glass windows.[4] Initially buying glass from other manufacturers, he subsequently hired various specialised furnaces to develop new types of glass which gave his windows added density and variety of colour and form.[5] The compositions were also innovative; they included landscapes, flowers, woods and streams, and involved new techniques to allow the glass to follow the organic lines of the subject matter. Tiffany windows were richly and densely coloured and highly complex. Their exhibition in Paris in 1894 marked the beginning of Tiffany's reputation as the foremost exponent of *Art Nouveau* in America.

The Secrets of Success

Tiffany's extraordinary success in his chosen field of the Decorative Arts was due to his determination to elevate the production of what were considered hum-drum, everyday objects to the level of Fine Art and his ability to take advantage of the enormous demand for new interiors after the end of the American Civil War. This success was not achieved on his own, however. Although he developed the design concepts, he did not make anything himself and his ability to attract, and retain, talented craftsmen, designers and technicians was crucial. Joseph Briggs was one of a number of people who worked with Tiffany for very long periods. Other key employees were Arthur Nash, with Tiffany from 1893 to 1924 and Clara Driscoll, the designer of most of Tiffany's leaded glass lampshades, from 1888 to 1909.[6] Mr R McLhenny, the chemist who arrived at the formula for creating iridescence in vase glass in 1894, was employed until Tiffany Furnaces closed in 1924. The men in the blowing shops remained largely the same over the 20 years of *Favrile* glass production. One was Jimmy Stewart, who admitted, "I liked my work - in fact, I loved it. Every piece was a beautiful thing. Every piece was out of this world."[7]

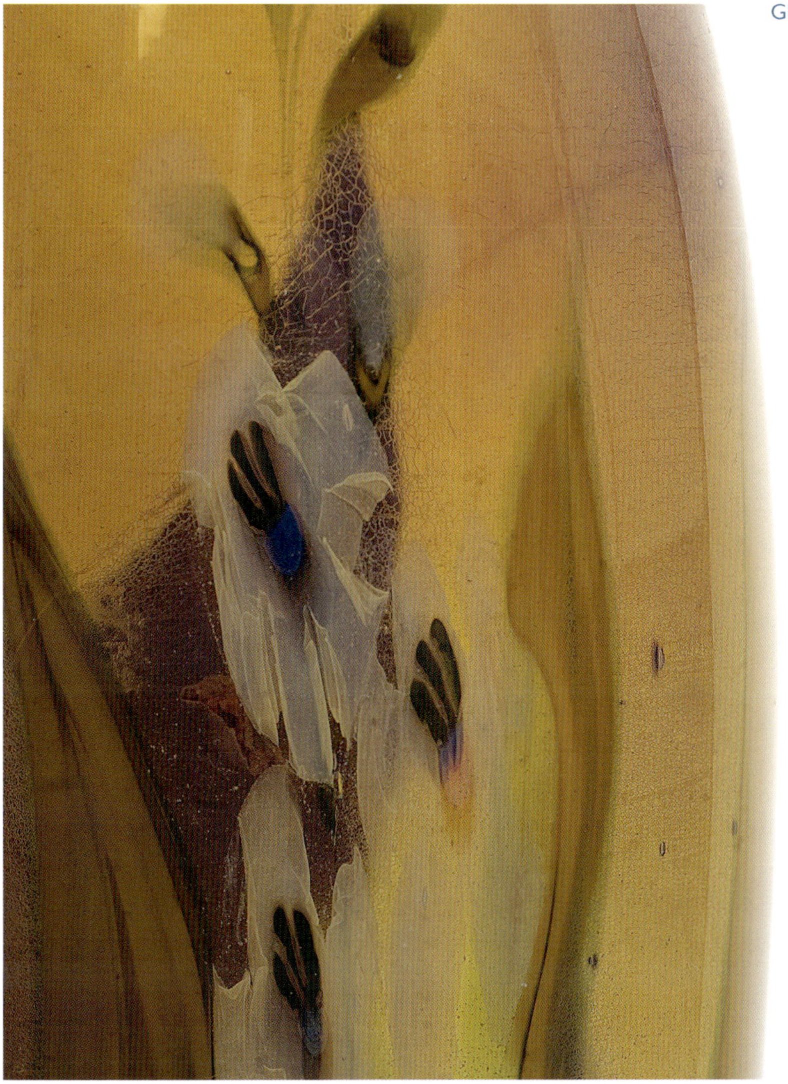

Gladiola Vase (detail)
cat. no. 44

Another key reason for Tiffany's success was his ability to virtually mass-produce objects which nevertheless retained a hand-made element of one sort or another. His desk-sets, for example, made of cast bronze and *Favrile* glass, were available in a dozen styles.[8] Even blown vases, where each was unique, were produced in a wide range of contrasting types of glass.[9] Tiffany Furnaces produced one-off vases in *Favrile* glass whilst also supplying the same glass for stained-glass windows, mosaics and lampshades. Aside from luxury items, available only to the wealthiest Americans, Tiffany also produced a wide range of glass tablewares and light fittings which were within the price-range of many more people.

Tiffany's enormous personal wealth enabled him to employ chemists and technicians to experiment for years, if necessary, in order to produce the colours and effects he wanted. He worked on a grand scale; in 1900 at the high point of Tiffany's success, he employed around 200 people who produced in that year around 20,000 *Favrile* glass vases and bowls. He paid his staff well in order to retain them; Clara Driscoll was amongst the highest-paid female designers in America. And, if despite the generous pay, former employees set up in competition with him, Tiffany had the means and resolution to use litigation to run them out of business. Indeed, Tiffany's wealth enabled him to continue the production of what were essentially 19th century artefacts in the *Art Nouveau* style, well in to the 20th century, when fashionable taste had moved on.

Favrile Glass: A Great Capacity for Beauty

Tiffany's recognition of the fact that glass had 'a great capacity for beauty' and his determination to demonstrate this, dominated his life through the late 1870s and 1880s.[10] An opportunity to develop his work in glass further occurred at the World's Columbian Exposition in 1893 where he head-hunted Arthur Nash (1849-1934), the manager of Thomas Webb and Sons, a Stourbridge glass works. Stourbridge, in England's West Midlands, had been at the forefront of innovation in the British glass industry for over 100 years. With Nash as supervisor of the new furnaces at the Tiffany Glass and Decorating Company, Tiffany devoted the next two years to continual experimentation to obtain the particular effects he wanted to see in his *Favrile* glass.

Patented in 1892 and unveiled to the world in Paris in 1894 and 1895, *Favrile* glass was radically different in its production from glass made by rival manufacturers because the decoration was created at the time of the blowing and forming of the vase. A 'gather,' or globule of glass, slightly inflated with air on the end of a blowpipe, would have a variety of coloured glass added to it. It would then be returned to the furnace to be re-heated and then worked on again with the addition of more glass. This elaborate process could be repeated as many as 20 times.[11] By combining the forming and decorating processes, Tiffany's glass-makers had to exert greater control over the glass in its more liquid state, resulting in a flowing, organic form of decoration which was always unique.

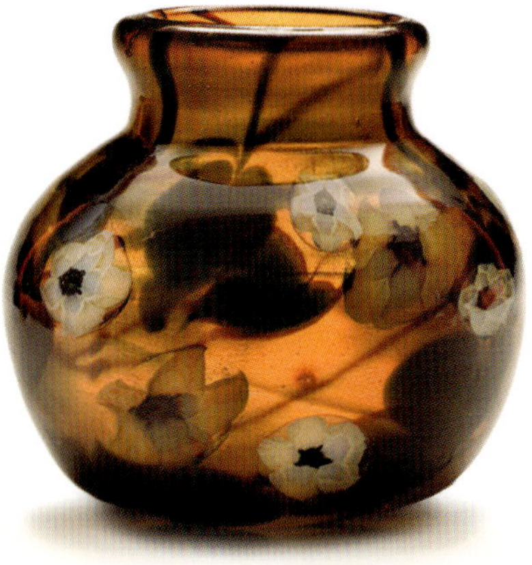

Millefiori **Paperweight Vase**
cat. no. 49

Tiffany Favrile Glass Advertisement, in
King's Photographic Views of New York, pg. 580, 1895.
Collection of the New-York Historical Society, negative #77532d

TIFFANY FAVRILE GLASS

· TIFFANY · GLASS · & · DECORATING · COMPANY ·

· FVRNISHERS · & · GLASS · WORKERS · DOMESTIC · & · ECCLESIASTICAL ·
DECORATIONS · GTD CO · MEMORIALS ·
· 333 · TO · 341 · FOVRTH · AVENVE · NEW · YORK ·

TIFFANY FAVRILE GLASS IS THE OUTCOME OF A SERIES OF EXPERIMENTS RECENTLY CONDUCTED BY MR. LOUIS C. TIFFANY. THE RESULT OF THESE INVESTIGATIONS IS SHOWN IN NEW COMBINATIONS OF COLOR WITH COLOR, COLOR OVER COLOR, THE DEEPENING OF TONE, THE SUBTLE QUALITY OF THE TEXTURE, THE INTRODUCTION OF NEW COLORS, THE UNION OF METAL WITH GLASS, AND THE WONDERFUL ORNAMENTAL EFFECTS OBTAINED BY IMBEDDING LINES AND THREADS OF ONE COLORED GLASS IN THAT OF ANOTHER, WHILE THEY ARE IN A MOLTEN STATE, AND DURING THE OPERATION OF BLOWING. TIFFANY FAVRILE GLASS HAS BEEN MADE INTO A VARIETY OF ORIGINAL FORMS IN VASES AND OTHER OBJECTS OF INTEREST TO COLLECTORS AND LOVERS OF ART. IT IS ALSO USED IN OUR FINER COLORED WINDOWS AND MOSAICS.

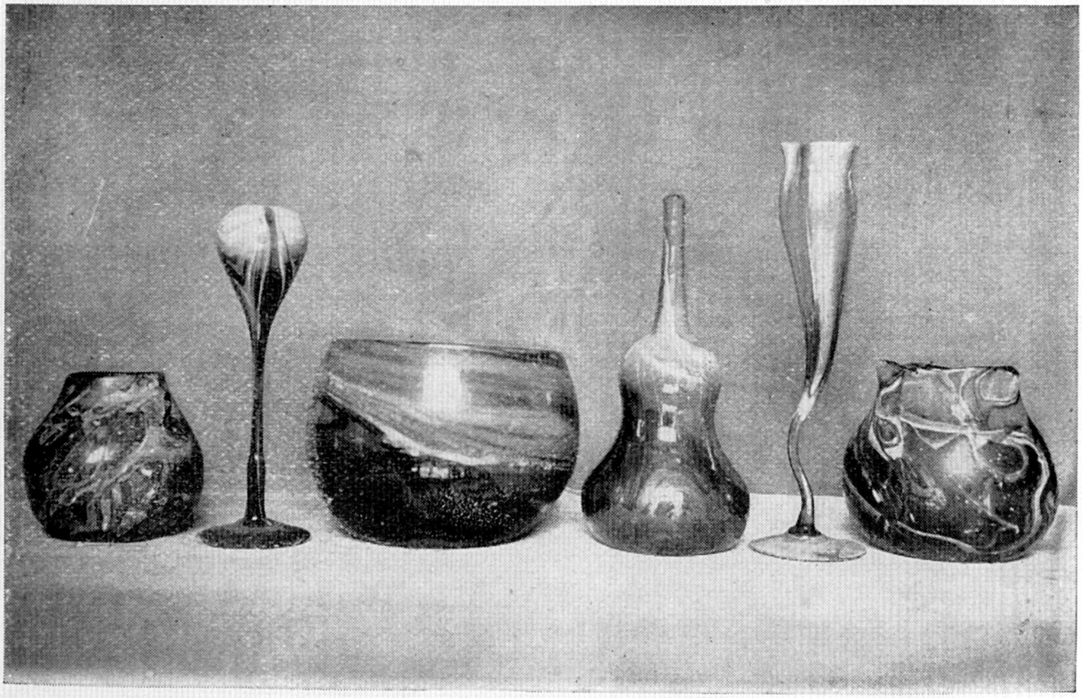

TIFFANY FAVRILE GLASS.

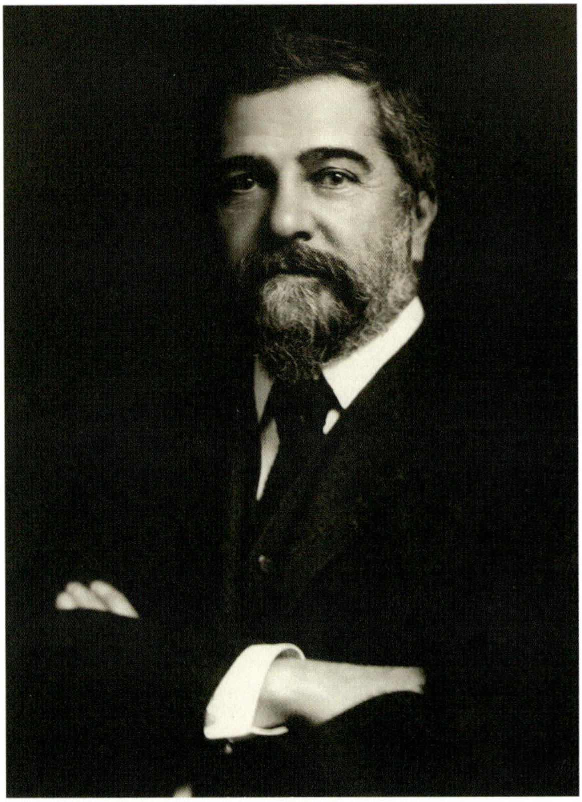

Louis Comfort Tiffany. Portrait by the Pach Brothers, no date. Collection of the New-York Historical Society, negative #49516.

Favrile glass was an immediate success. It had become the perfect vehicle for Tiffany to express his love of the natural world, with its infinite variety of forms and ever-changing colours and moods. Samuel Bing, the Parisian art critic and dealer, excitedly displayed *Favrile* glass vases in his 1895 *Salon de L'Art Nouveau.* He praised Tiffany because his new glass showed that, "After all the accomplishments of the Venetians, of Gallé and others, it was still possible to innovate, to utilize glass in a new way."[12]

The radical new look of Tiffany's *Favrile* glass can be seen in all of the vases in the Haworth's collection, with the exception of those where glass cutting is the main means of decoration. But even the latter have a fluidity of line and an organic quality that belies the inflexibility of the decorating process. *Favrile* glass is a dramatic symbol of Tiffany's loyalty to the Arts and Crafts notion of allowing the essential nature of the material to be wholly evident in the finished object. This loyalty is the single most important reason behind Tiffany's pre-eminence as the master of *Art Nouveau* glass-making.

---

1 From Tiffany's lecture 'The Quest of Beauty' given 18 February 1916. Quoted in *Louis C Tiffany: The Collected Works of Robert Koch,* 2001. p.329.

2 Like many of his wealthy contemporaries, Tiffany was inspired by the art of other cultures; he became a collector of Japanese, Chinese and Native American art.

3 The Mark Twain House and Museum opened to the public in 2003. The Armory, on Park Avenue, is a venue for alternative arts events, exhibitions and antiques fairs. The massive fireplace is made of hundreds of turquoise iridescent tiles like those in the Haworth's collection.

4 A complete list of all Tiffany's stained-glass windows has never been produced, although Tiffany Studios published lists in 1896 and 1910.

5 Tiffany made drapery glass in 1877 at Thill's Flint glass works and opalescent and iridescent glass in 1881 at Louis Heildt and Company's furnace.

6 Arthur J Nash was manager of Tiffany Furnaces from 1902. Clara Driscoll had two breaks in her employment as she married twice and was ineligible for work as a married woman.

7 Stewart talking in an interview with Robert Koch, 6th April 1966, quoted in his book *Louis C Tiffany's Glass-Bronzes-Lamps,* 1971, pp 62-73.

8 The styles the 26 piece Tiffany desk set was available in were: Adam, Abalone, American Indian, Bookmark, Byzantine, Chinese, Graduate, Grapevine, Nautical, Pine-Needle, Venetian and Zodiac.

9 *Favrile* glass vases were made in Tiffany's five blowing shops, usually consisting of a gaffer or master blower, a server, a decorator, a gatherer, a mixer and two boys helping. The types of *Favrile* glass vases produced included: Agate, Aquamarine, Cameo, Cypriote , Intaglio, Iridescent, Lava, *Millefiori,* Paperweight and Reactive.

10 Quoted as (1) above.

11 Stewart gave this description of the process in the Koch interview quoted as (7) above.

12 Quoted in *Louis C Tiffany: The Collected Works of Robert Koch,* 2001, p.94.

Life of Louis Comfort Tiffany

1848	Born on 18 February in New York, the second son of Charles Tiffany (1812-1902), founder of Tiffany & Co, Silversmiths and Jewellers.
1865/66	First visit to Europe, aged 17 years.
1868/9	Studied painting in Paris with Orientalist painters.
1870	Eight-month journey to Europe and North Africa.
1875/7	Earliest experiments in glass-making.
1879/80	Earliest interior design commissions.
1881	Sucessfully obtained three glass-making patents.
1883	LC Tiffany and Company is formed.
1889	Travelled extensively in Europe.
1892	Formed the Tiffany Glass and Decorating Company and established his own glass-house at Corona.
1893	Tiffany pieces won 54 medals at Chicago World's Columbian Exposition.
1894	Registered the *Favrile* trademark for his glass.
1894	Exhibited 10 *Favrile* glass windows at the *Salon du Champ de Mars,* Paris
1895	*Favrile* glass vases exhibited at the *Salon de L'Art Nouveau,* Paris.
1900	Tiffany enjoyed phenomenal success at the International Exhibition in Paris and was awarded the *Legion d'Honneur.* Tiffany Glass and Decorating Company became Tiffany Studios.
1902	Appointed Art Director of Tiffany & Co, Silversmiths and Jewellers, on the death of his father. Tiffany Furnaces set up at Corona.
1902/5	Building of sumptuous country house Laurelton Hall near Oyster Bay, Long Island, New York.
1916	Exhibition of Tiffany's paintings and *Favrile* glass to mark his 68th Birthday.
1918	Resigned as Art Director of Tiffany and Co, and appointed Joseph Briggs to run Tiffany Studios and Arthur Nash to run Tiffany Furnaces.
1919	LC Tiffany Foundation established to support young artists with a $1million donation from Tiffany.
1924	Tiffany Furnaces dissolved.
1932	Tiffany Studios declared bankrupt. The Louis C Tiffany Studios Corporation formed to continue its activities with Tiffany as President and Art Director.
1933	17 January, died of pneumonia in New York aged 84 years.

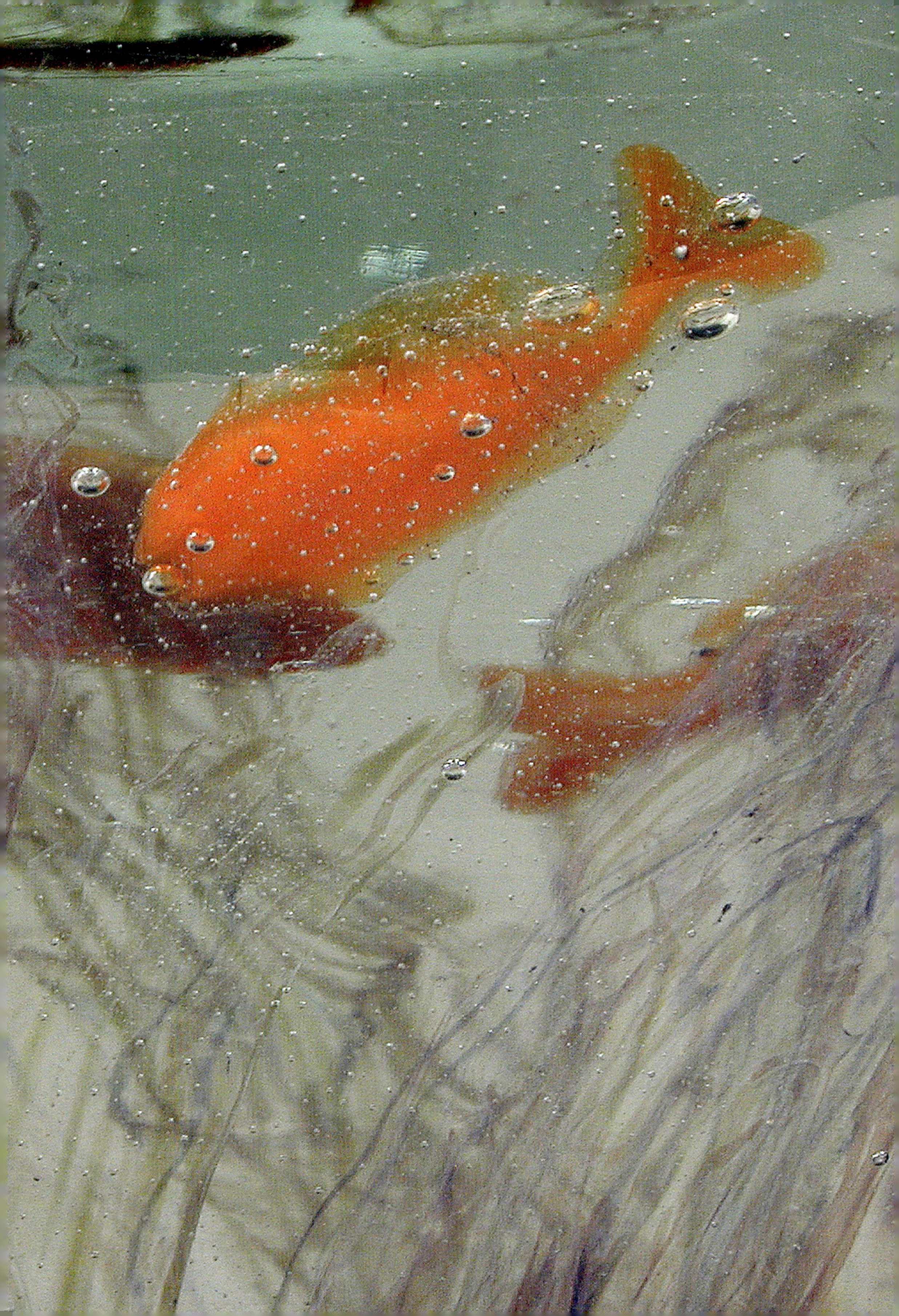

Layering Colours: Tiffany *Favrile* vases

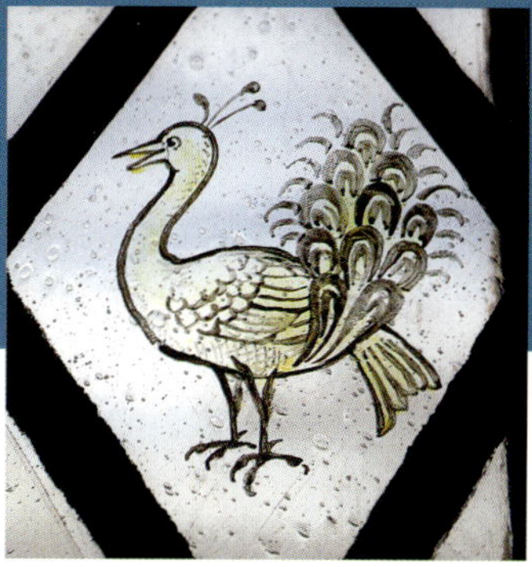

Louis Comfort Tiffany was first and foremost a painter. Privately tutored by the landscape painter George Inness (1825-1894), he associated in the 1860s with the Hudson River painters of New York. Although in tune with their romanticised landscapes, Tiffany disliked the fashionable large-scale compositions of the time and so looked elsewhere for ways to express his emotional attachment to the natural world. During the 1870s he turned increasingly to interior design and began working directly with glass. Tiffany increased his experimentation with the use of colour in glass tiles and windows during the 1880s but it was only after 1892 when the Tiffany Glass and Decorating Company was formed that this work became a major focus for him.

Tiffany never fully abandoned painting but it was through the medium of free-blown glass that he began arguably the most satisfying and successful period of his creative life. From early on in his production of *Favrile* glass, traditional vase shapes gave way to more organic designs inspired by vegetables, fruit and flowers, their decorations echoing and enhancing these freer forms. Tiffany's vases are works of art in their own right, curved glass canvases across which fabulous colours are dispersed. They were all signed like paintings; they were the products of an artist in his studio and they elevated the production of what were essentially domestic objects to the status of Fine Art.

A close look at eight of the Haworth's superb collection of *Favrile* vases reveals the success of Tiffany's painterly approach to glass, where the glass surface is treated like a canvas and light and dark, surface texture and depth are all compositional elements. The Peacock vase, Flower and Onion Form vases, have fine veils of transparent, opaque and iridescent colours displayed across their surfaces. The surface of the Lava vase is worked into and built up to create a more three-dimensional effect. In the Rose vase, more depth is created through deep cutting into the glass and in the Cameo vase, layers of colour are manipulated to reveal a different, more subtle penetration. Paperweight glass encases the Gladiola vase, suspending tiny flowers in real space. This embedding process is pushed even further in the Aquamarine, where glass masquerades as water in which goldfish swim amongst air bubbles and water-weed.

Arts and Crafts motif:
Peacock (top), staircase window, Haworth Art Gallery (not Tiffany)

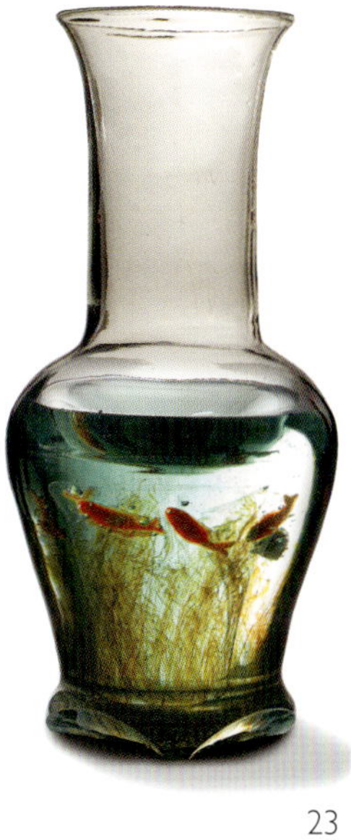

Aquamarine Vase
(detail opposite)
cat. no. 51

Peacock Vase

The Peacock Vase is a classic of Tiffany's *Favrile* glass production and its iridescent Peacock feather emblematic of the *Art Nouveau* movement. Tiffany's development and perfection of iridescent glass was arguably his single most important achievement.[1] Iridescent colours had been applied successfully by Tiffany to the lime glass used for stained-glass windows. However, the red lead glass used for vases required a different formula and experimentation by a succession of four different chemists continued non-stop for two years from 1893 until 1895, when, finally, "we made the first vase of Tiffany iridescent glass."[2] This breakthrough gave Tiffany and his workers the confidence to throw themselves whole-heartedly into creating more and more fabulous and unusual effects in their glass.

George J Cook developed the formula for the Peacock feather motif, which was one of the most difficult and prized *Favrile* glass designs. He used opaque, transparent and aventurine glass to create the five distinctive types of glass required.[3] Rods of this subtly varied glass were drawn across the body of the vase to create the delicate yet pliable fronds of the feather.

The resulting striations, which flicker with silvery pink, mauve and blue lights, have the fleeting quality of iridescence in nature. The silvery or opalescent 'eyes' of the feathers, inserted amongst these striations, complete the representation of one of the natural world's most beautiful creations.

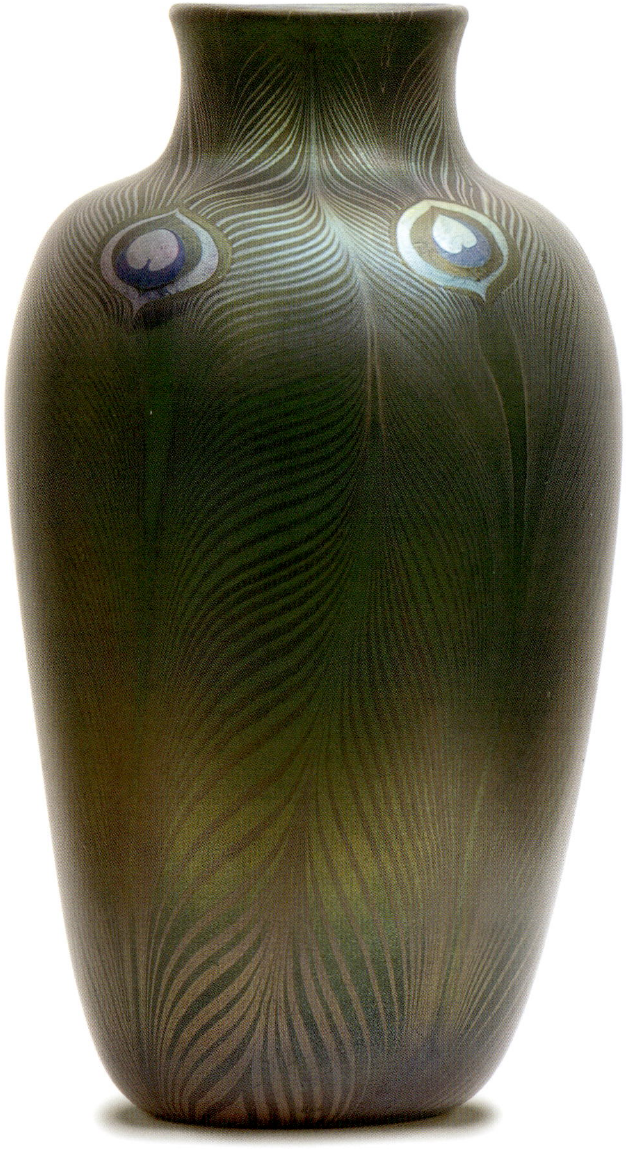

Peacock Vase
cat. no. 2

Flower Form Vase

The Flower Form vase represents a radical move away from the traditional vase shape by the Tiffany Glass and Decorating Company. The type was created by Tiffany's first master glass-blower, Tom Manderson, in the mid-1890s and the name describes it exactly, that is, a vase which takes the form of a flower.[4]

The Haworth example is inspired by the Field Bindweed or Convulvulus.[5] Arthur Nash developed the design which was made in two parts, the head and stem being blown separately from the foot. The blossom has an irregular waving edge full of movement, a reminder that the Convolvulus opens in daylight and closes at night. Filaments of green and pink glass run across it to describe petals and sepals, while the ribbed stem recalls the bindweed's fine entwining tendrils. The domed foot of the vase approximates the leaves and the blossom is coloured with the glorious rose pinks and golds of the skies around the setting sun. Tiffany went on to produce a great variety of Flower Forms which were extremely popular by 1900. They remain masterpieces of *Art Nouveau* glass.

The Flower Form was an important early *Favrile* glass creation, demonstrating that Tiffany's glass-makers could adopt radical shapes that showed off the spectacular colour effects being created. The Jack-in-the-Pulpit vase (cat. no. 52) is another variation of the type, where the blossom is opened further and turned on its side to show off its luminous iridescence to greatest effect.

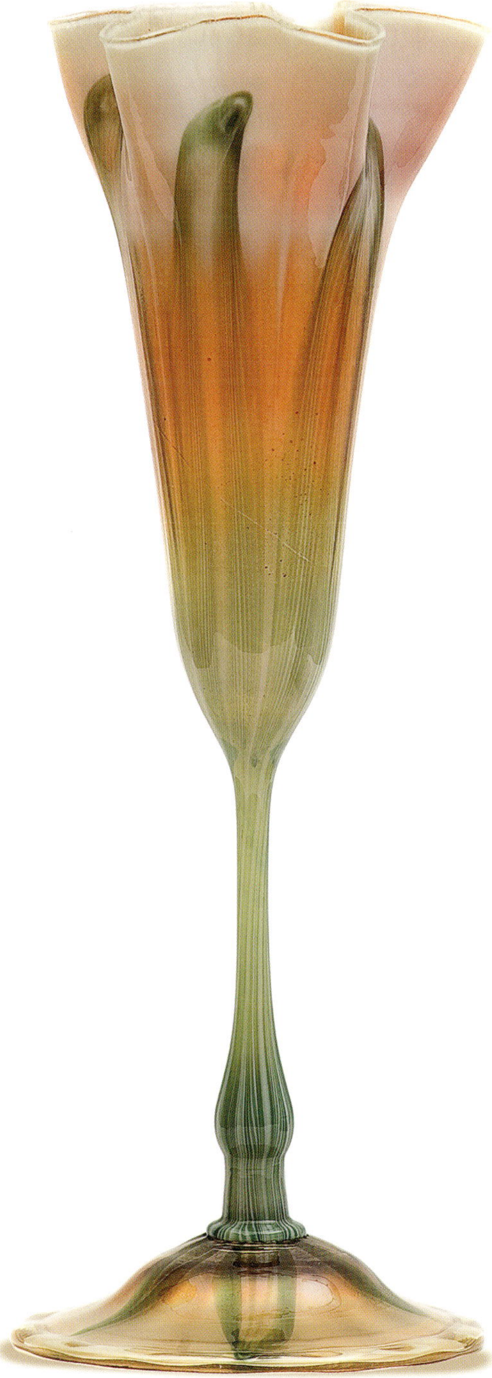

Flower Form Vase
cat. no. 4

Onion Form Vase

This spectacular and rare example of *Favrile* glass is so called because the base of the vase is shaped like an onion. The prosaic name belies its fabulously elegant black glass body, decorated with six 'teardrops' of startlingly luminous iridescent colour. Tiffany may have been inspired by 16th century Persian vessels which were used as rosewater sprinklers, or to collect the tears of a loved one. Examples of these were displayed at New York's Metropolitan Museum of Art. Islamic art was a major influence on Tiffany after his first visit to North Africa in 1870. The heat and colour inspired him and the atmospheric glowing of glass lamps in the Great Mosque in Cairo made a lasting impression.

The use of vegetable forms with their irregular geometry was typical of the *Art Nouveau* movement. Other vases in the Haworth collection reflect this interest in the asymmetry of nature and demonstrate Tiffany's radical approach to the production of free-blown glass vases. See, for example, catalogue number 50, a black vase with a gourd-like form and catalogue numbers 21 and 27, Lava vases with uneven, lumpy profiles reminiscent of potatoes.

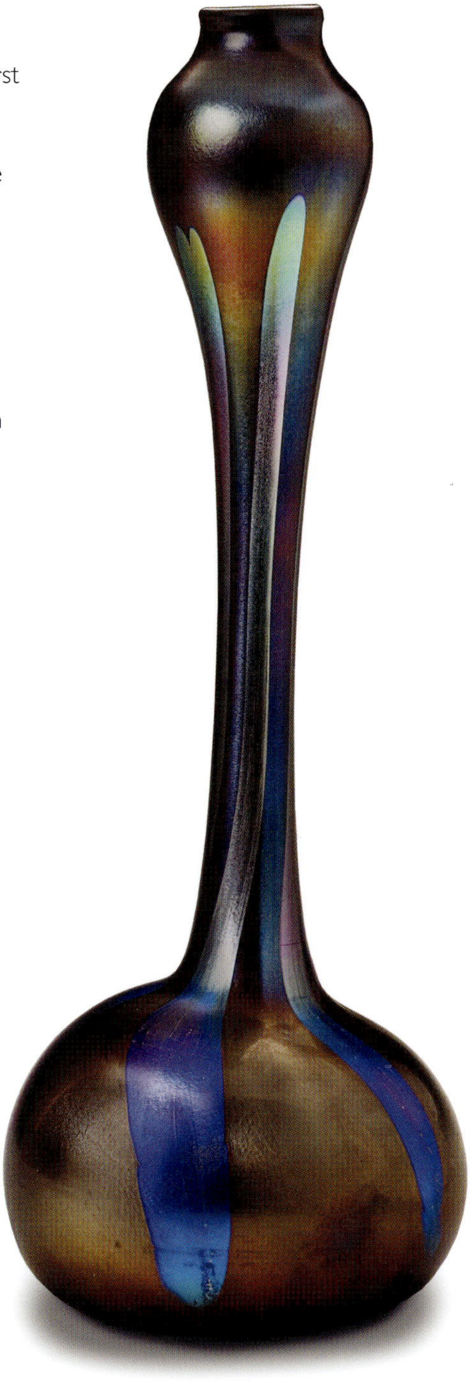

Onion Form Vase
(detail opposite)
cat. no. 6

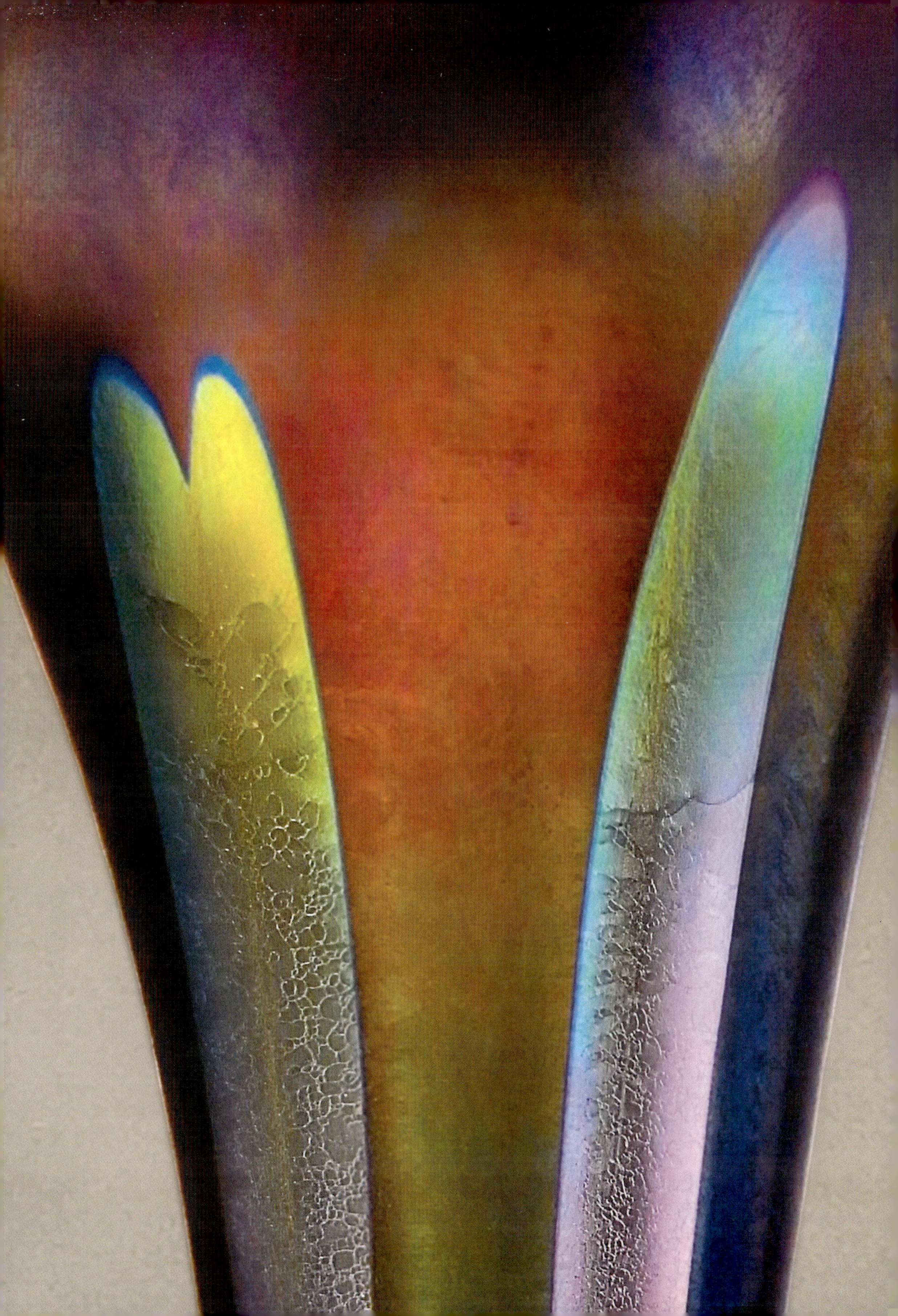

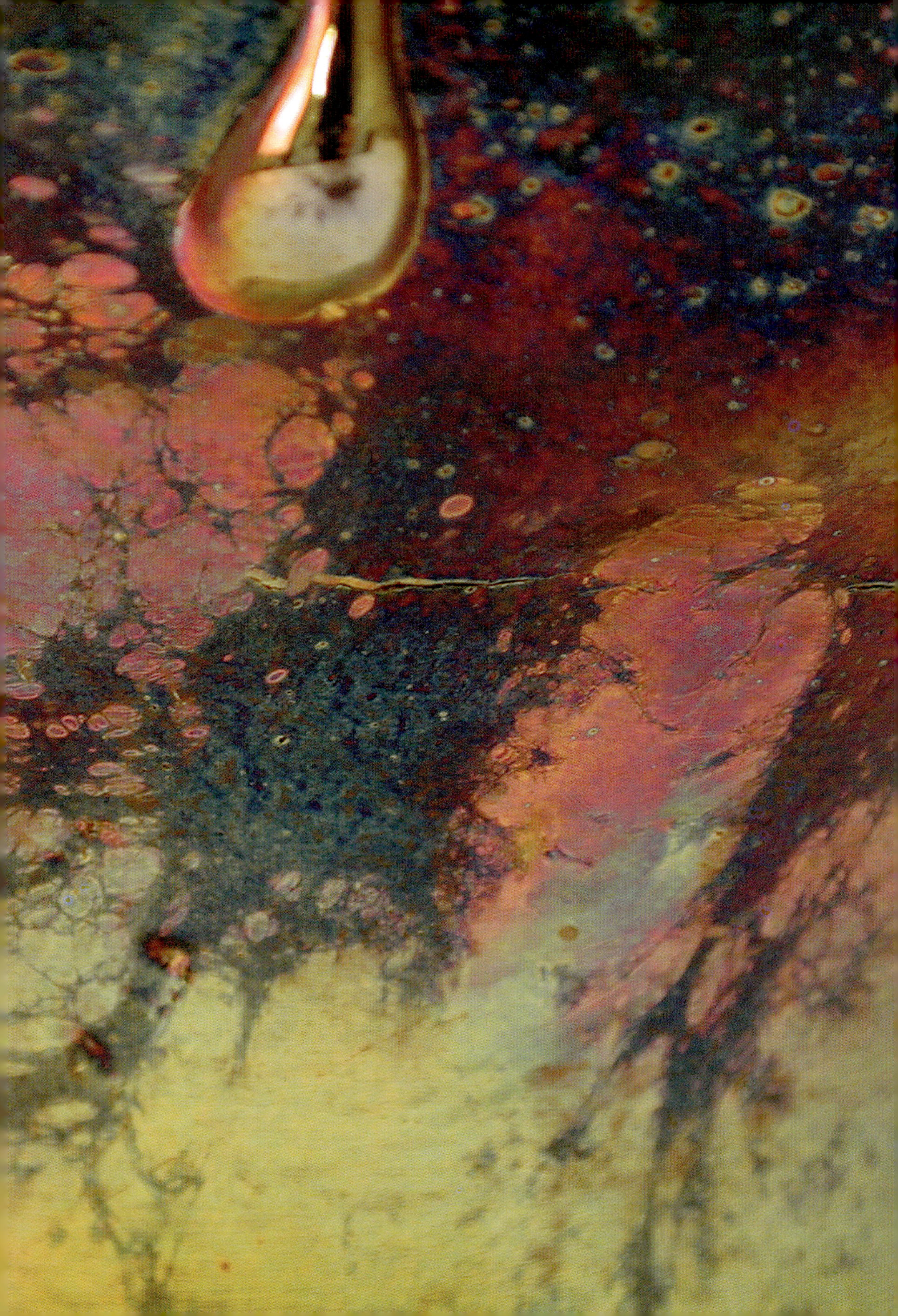

Lava Vase

The Lava vase belongs to the Cypriote group of vases, a name created by Tiffany himself.[6] Always opaque, Cypriotes have a rough, pitted surface, sometimes showing burst air bubbles. This effect was achieved by rolling the *gather* or globule of glass to be blown across the *marver* or flat surface which had been covered with tiny fragments of the same glass. Once blown into its final, classically simple shape, iridescent colours were applied to the surface.

Amongst the most abstract of Tiffany's work, Lava glass, also known as Volcanic glass, is intended to remind the viewer of an erupting volcano, the rim of the vase suggesting its mouth. Lava vases were costly, difficult to make and less popular. However, they were a favourite of Tiffany's. He probably prided himself on using such an ambitious idea for a mere vase and demonstrating that his glass-makers could free themselves so completely from tradition. To achieve the rough, lumpy texture of Lava glass, basalt or talc was added to the molten glass before blowing. Later in the process, additional glass was applied and fused into the body of the vase and finally the surfaces were lustred with gold.

In Rome in February 1866, Tiffany had visited archaeological sites and seen ancient glass vessels being unearthed, their surfaces fractured by salts, having been buried for thousands of years. He no doubt also visited the Metropolitan Museum of Art in New York, where newly acquired, partly decomposed Roman vessels from Cyprus were attracting public attention.[7] It is well-known that the curious rough surfaces and iridescent effects of this glass inspired Tiffany to achieve similar effects in his own glass.

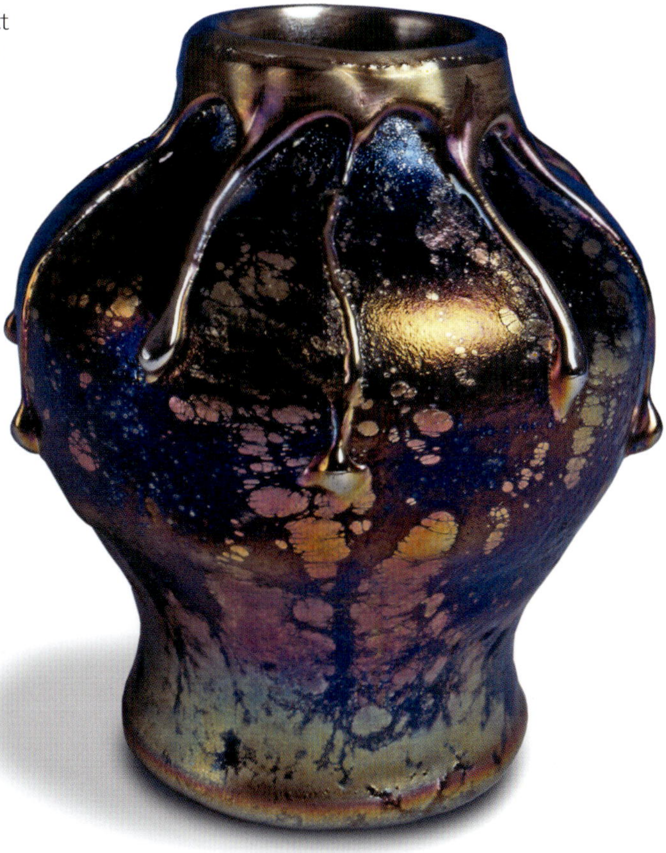

Lava Vase
(detail opposite)
cat. no. 27

Rose Vase

The informality and freedom of the form and decoration of many of the vases in the Haworth collection imitate the liquidity of glass. This is not the case with the Rose vase. Here the glass is mastered utterly and transformed into a complex depiction of a Rose in its various stages of growth, from bud to full bloom. The technique used to decorate the vase is the closest Tiffany came to traditional cut glass, in which lead crystal glass is refined and clarified to such a fine degree before it is blown, that when cut it sparkles like diamonds.

Tiffany introduced the type of frosted opalescent glass used for the Rose vase, which has the appearance of Moonstone, around 1903. The Rose vase is a *tour-de-force* of the *intaglio* cutting technique in which the decoration is cut away while at the same time leaving the surface plane of the vessel clearly visible. The glass was blown, left to cool slowly then engraved with a rotating copper wheel. Unusually for an *intaglio* vase, it has a faint lustre, achieved by spraying the inside with chemicals. This type is well documented in the notebooks of Tiffany's furnaces manager Arthur Nash, who recorded a similar vase taking 181 hours to cut.[8]

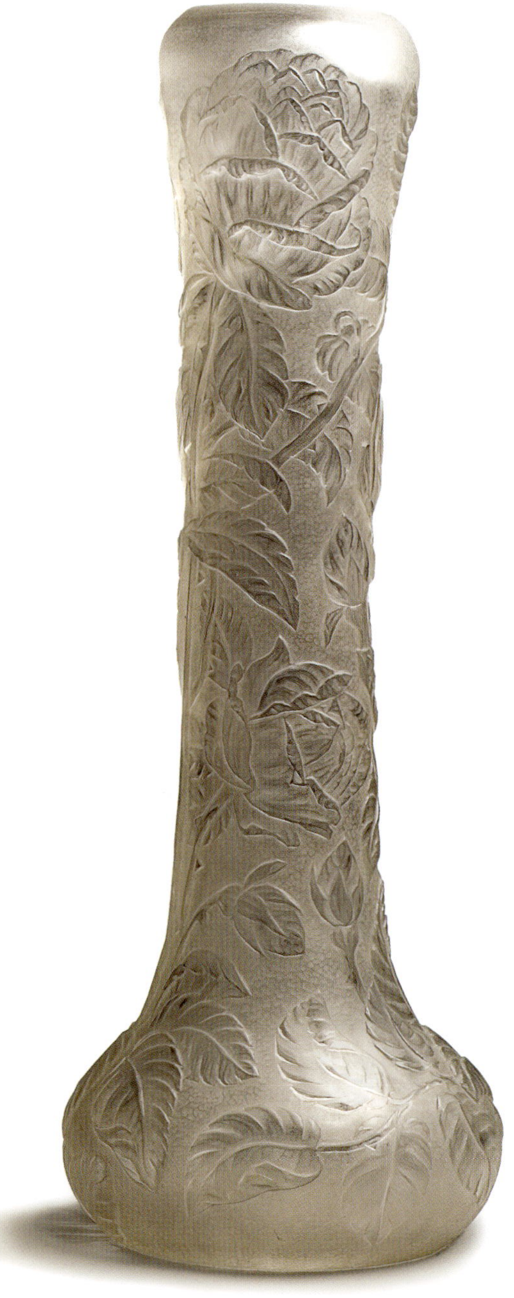

Rose Vase
cat. no. 28

Cameo Vase

The Cameo glass technique is an ancient technique which was developed by Roman and Alexandrian craftsmen around 100 BC.[9] It involves layering at least two different colours of glass one on top of the other. After blowing the vase is cooled and cut back in relief with a wheel. Tiffany's French contemporary Emile Gallé (1846-1904) developed the technique in many new directions although Tiffany also used it extensively.[10]

This quietly beautiful little vase is made of three layers of glass, first a transparent layer, then a pink and then a green. It was blown into a mould to achieve the subtle flatness of the five green leaves encasing the ten pink petals. The layers were then carved to describe a flower, probably a Lily. The complexity and sophistication of the carving contrasts with the simplicity of the tiny cuts which define the top of the vase. This latter decoration draws attention to the transparent glass on which the flower is carved. It is as if, without this, we might mistakenly think we were looking at nature, not artifice.

A related use of coloured layers of glass by Tiffany glass-makers is found in Agate glass, where a variety of opaque coloured glasses are stirred together. After the blowing and cooling of the vase it was cut in facets to show off the coloured layers which are like those found in the semi-precious stone Agate. Catalogue number 42 is a stunning example.

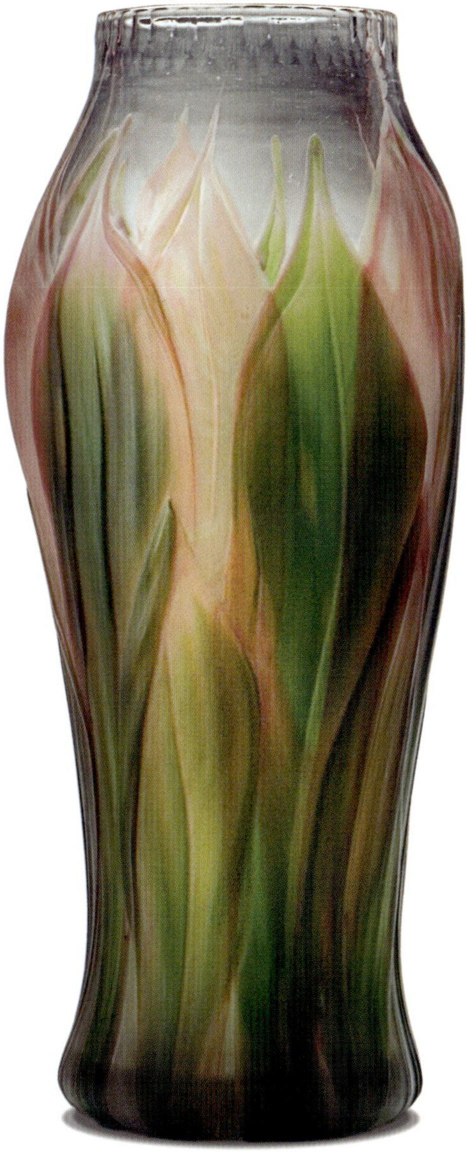

Cameo Vase
cat. no. 10

Gladiola Vase

This superb vase demonstrates Tiffany's adherence to the 'truth to materials' ideal of the Arts and Crafts movement of the 19th century. The decoration of the vase and its forming were achieved simultaneously and the essential nature of the material, that is, the fluidity of the glass, is evident in the finished vase. The creation of the Gladiola vase, achieved mainly by blowing, also involved a complex series of additions to, and manipulations of, the glass both in and out of the furnace. The 'gather' of transparent, iridescent glass was decorated with the elegant lime green leaves by the addition of pads of glass which grew as the glass was blown. The ten blooms which decorate the vase further, were cut from a pre-formed cane of many fine rods of glass and adhered to the 'gather' with drops of molten glass. A final layer of transparent glass was then added and the blowing completed.

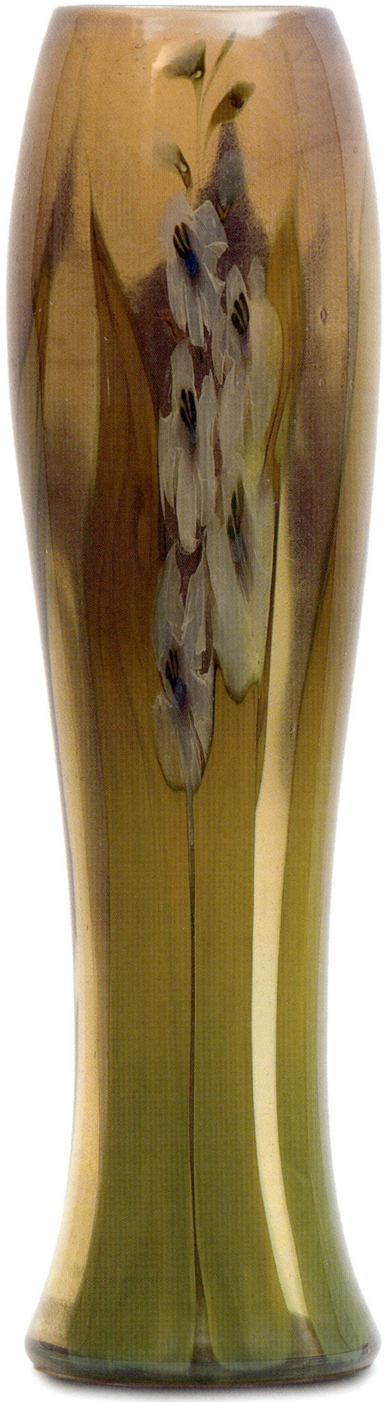

This technique has been described as *millefiori* paperweight, though Tiffany himself did not use the term. *Millefiori* means many flowers and paperweight refers to the final, encasing 'gather' of transparent glass which gives the vase its shiny finish.[11] Catalogue numbers 13, 14, 48, 49 and 67 are further examples of this type and catalogue number 9 has 50 tiny flowers dispersed across its surface. Catalogue number 49, decorated with Morning Glory flowers, shows the layering of this technique very clearly. The first group of white flowers added to the 'gather' appear beige, because they were embedded under a subsequent gather of orange glass and are stretched out of shape by blowing. The second group, added later in the process, remain white because they were embedded under the transparent paperweight glass and are more regular in shape because they were subject to less blowing.

Gladiola Vase
cat. no. 44

Aquamarine Vase

Also known as 'Underwater glass,' the Aquamarine is a mass of solid glass, masquerading as a water-filled vase containing water-weed and six goldfish. Aquamarines are few in number and usually much smaller than this exceptionally rare example because of the challenging technical and time constraints involved in producing them. A great deal of careful temperature control over long periods was needed to prevent the pre-formed, press-moulded glass fish exploding as they were being embedded into the molten glass.

The Haworth Aquamarine was made in two stages, indicated by the water-weed that sits in two concentric circles. A fist shape of transparent, sea-green glass was formed and decorated with trails of glass to represent water-weed. Then the six press-moulded goldfish were inserted in to a rectangular mass of molten glass of the same colour which was then annealed around the fist shape and decorated with more trails of glass. It has been suggested that in a third stage, in order to make the neck of the vase, molten transparent paperweight glass was attached to the Aquamarine and then spun on an industrial lathe.[12] When finally cold, the base of the Aquamarine was cut with indentations which were then filled with brown and green glass to indicate mossy pebbles. This extraordinary type is representative of the most elaborate *Favrile* glass developed by Tiffany and the Haworth example, also remarkable for its large size, is the most successful of the very few Aquamarine vases with goldfish known to exist.

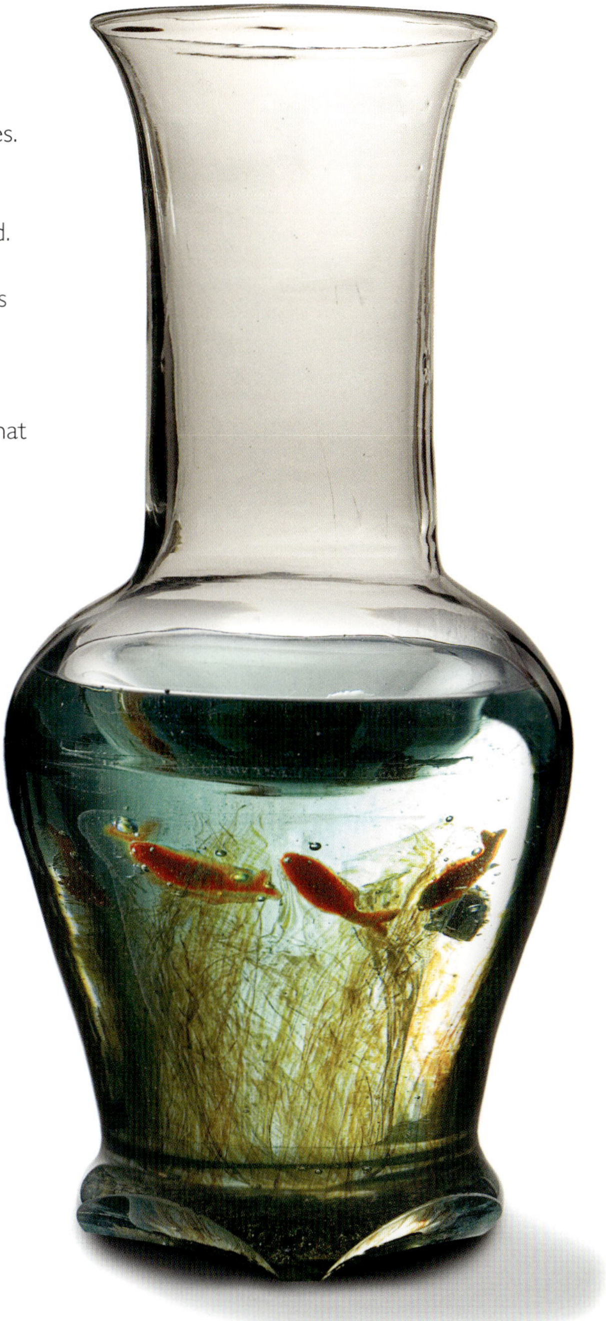

Aquamarine Vase
cat. no. 51

1 Iridescent glass re-created the rainbow colours seen fleetingly on a peacock feather or the wing of a dragonfly or starling. The colours change depending on the angle of the light source or the position of the viewer. Other glassmakers made iridescent glass before Tiffany but he perfected the effect, making it softer and more natural. It was achieved by introducing metallic substances in to the batch of glass or by spraying the cooled glass surface with chlorides and re-heating it.

2 Gaffer Jimmy Stewart recalled everyone dancing with joy at their success. Interview with Robert Koch, 6 April 1966 in his book *Louis C Tiffany's Glass-Bronzes-Lamps*, 1971, pp 62-73.

3 Aventurine glass was translucent and incorporated flecks of oxidised gold or copper.

4 19th century glass-makers had already produced similarly-shaped vases in Venice and Stourbridge.

5 Tiffany loved wild flowers; his Long Island home Laurelton Hall had many acres of wild flower meadows tended by large numbers of gardeners.

6 The name Cypriote indicated ancient and described iridescent vases with a simple, classical shape and a more or less rough, irregular surface. There are nine in the Haworth collection: catalogue numbers 3, 19, 21, 27, 56, 59, 64, 65, and 66.

7 New Yorker De Cesnold led an archaeological dig to Cyprus in search of ancient Aegean treasures but unearthed a large number of partly decomposed Roman glass vessels instead. They were displayed in the Metropolitan Museum of Art. Tiffany named his Cypriote glass after them.

8 Eidelberg, M. et al. *Behind the Scenes of Tiffany Glassmaking: The Nash Notebooks.* New York, 2001; pp 66-7.

9 The Portland Vase, in the British Museum, London, is the most famous example of the Cameo technique in glass-making. The technique developed out of the practice of cutting through the coloured layers of agate and other semi-precious stones to make jewellery, from around 300 BC.

10 Tiffany was inspired and challenged by the Gallé glass at the 1893 World's Columbian Exposition.

11 Glass canes for making *Millefiori* flowers were pre-formed and ranged in diameter from a few millimetres to eight or nine centimetres. Tiny slivers of the canes were cut and adhered to the glass during the blowing process. Paperweight glass was highly transparent and when used as the final 'gather' of glass, gave the vase a shiny 'underwater' finish.

12 These explanations were given to J Rennie by two practising glass-makers from 'World of Glass' in St Helens, UK and a retired engineer from an industrial glass background.

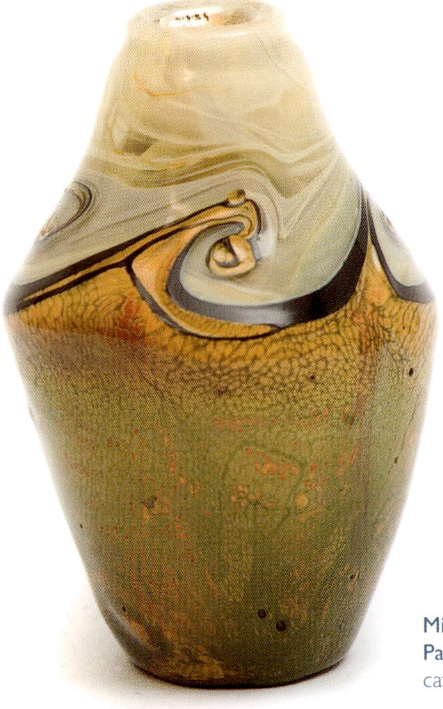

Miniature Paperweight Vase
cat. no. 54

Rose Vase
(detail)
cat. no. 28

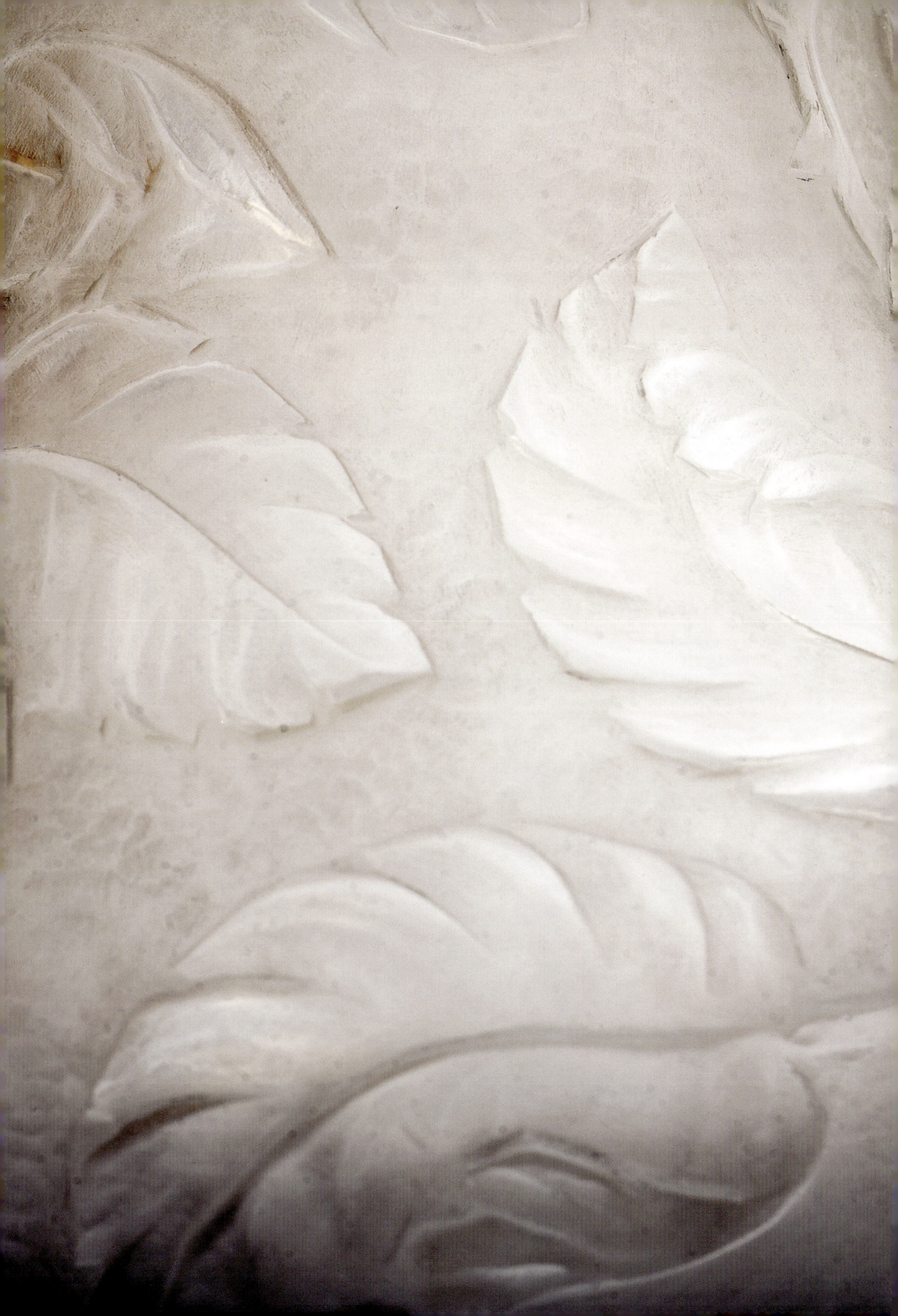

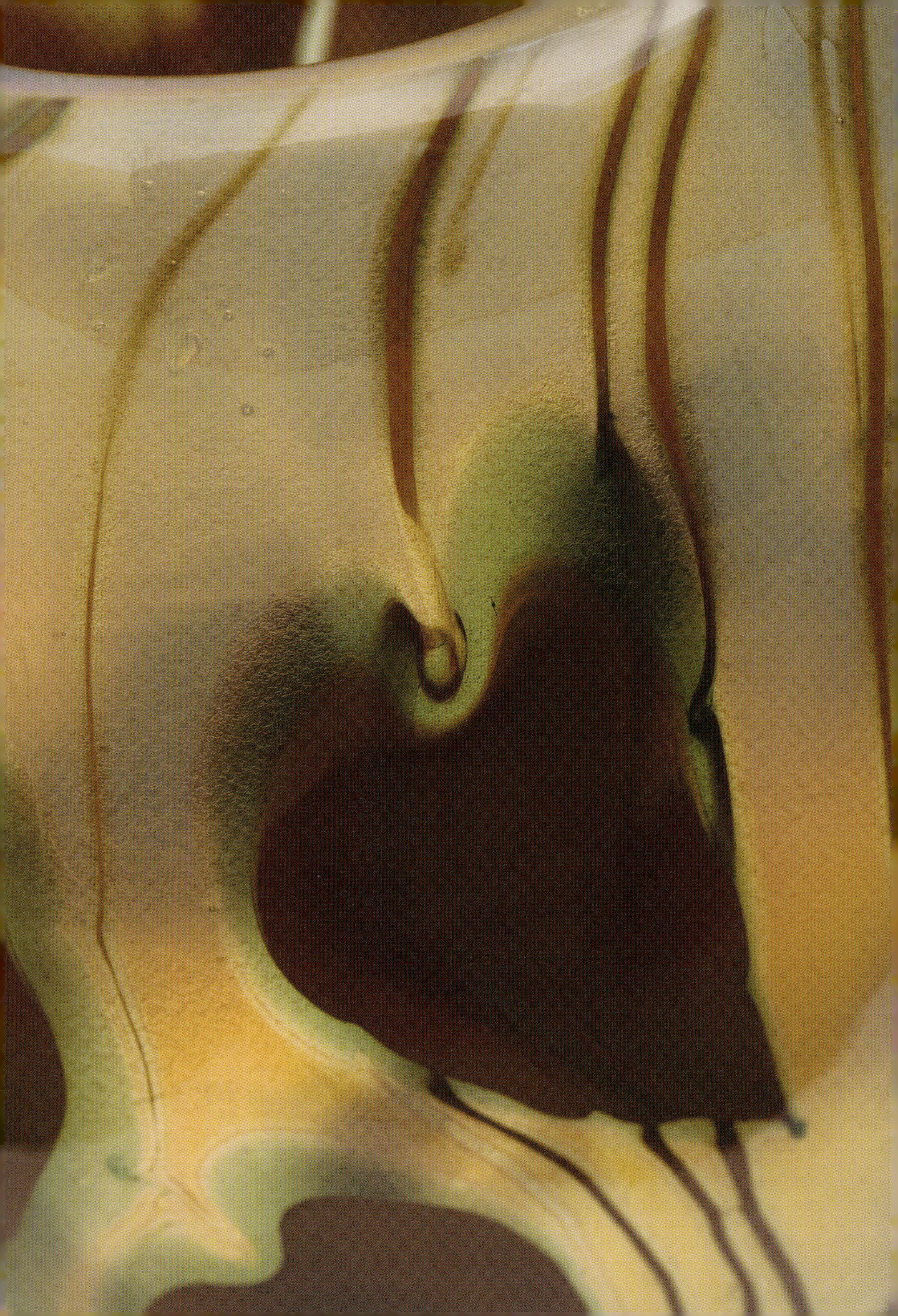

Catalogue of the Haworth Art Gallery's Tiffany Collection

All pieces were given by Joseph Briggs and the Briggs Family of Milnshaw Lane, Accrington in 1932 and 1933, unless otherwise stated.

The Haworth's *Favrile* vases are listed in the order of manufacture suggested by Martin Eidelberg's analysis of the Tiffany *Favrile* vase numbering system, with its use of prefixes and suffixes, found engraved on the base of each vase. This is given in his book *Tiffany Favrile Glass and the Quest of Beauty,* New York, 2007. In accordance with this analysis, the bulk of the Haworth's vases, catalogue numbers 10 to 50, were made between 1900 and 1910. Catalogue numbers 1 to 9 date from between 1895 and 1900, numbers 51 to 56 to the 1910 to 1915 period and the remainder date from 1926 onwards. However, this is only a rough guide to date of manufacture; there are anomalies and inconsistencies in the numbering system and experts disagree about its meaning and importance.

'Engraved' denotes the engraved inscription found on the base of the vase. All engraved signatures and numbers with a prefix or suffix are given in the catalogue entry. Reference is made to trademark labels: TGDC, for the Tiffany Glass and Decorating Company, used from 1892 and LCT, for Louis Comfort Tiffany, used from 1902 to 1919. All measurements are height before width, a single measurement indicating height only.

In 1999, Hamburg's Museum für Kunst und Gewerbe (Museum of Applied Arts) presented the first major exhibition in Europe devoted to Tiffany's work, to mark the 150th anniversary of his birth. Entitled *Louis C Tiffany - Masterpieces of American Art Nouveau,* it included 28 pieces from the Accrington collection. These are denoted in this catalogue with 'Hamburg, 1999', followed by the catalogue number in brackets.

Literary references to the Collection are too numerous to include here. A book list is available from the Haworth on request.

The Haworth accession number, where allocated, beginning 1999.33, is given in square brackets.

The number at the end of each entry is the Haworth display number.

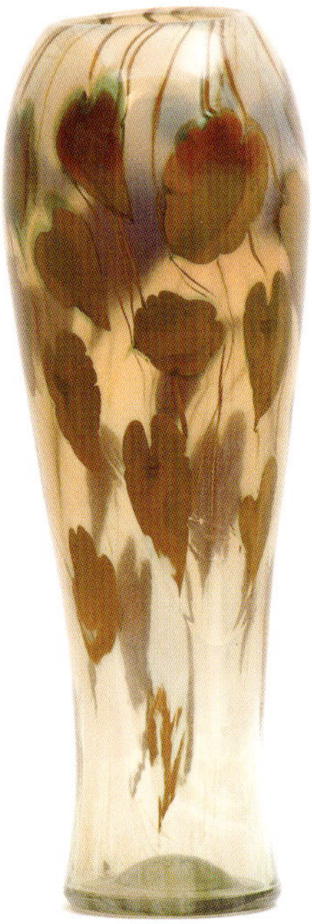

Paperweight Vase
(detail opposite)
cat. no. 47

Favrile Glass Vases

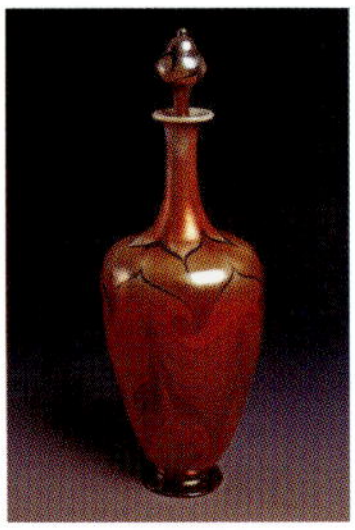

1 Carafe

Marbleised iridescent orange glass with feathered decoration (Decoration made by laying threads of glass on to the molten surface and combing them). 33 cm.
Engraved: L.C.Tiffany D 947 Favrile
With original black and white TGDC label and $40 price label.
Exhibited: Hamburg, 1999 (no. 82)
[inv.1999.33.34ab] 35

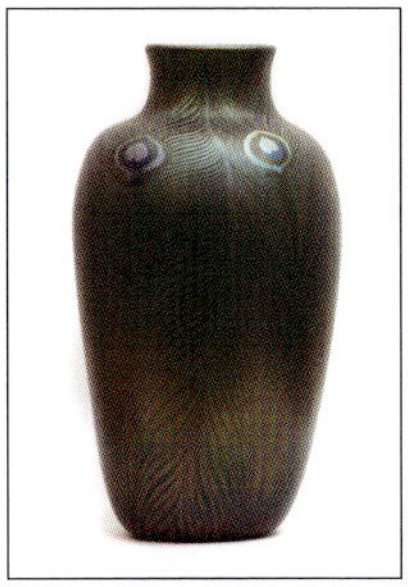

2 Peacock Vase

Monumental green glass vase with iridescent decoration in the form of five Peacock feathers. 48 cm.
Engraved: L.C.Tiffany-Favrile/ F 1977
With original black and white TGDC label.
Exhibited: Hamburg, 1999 (no. 108); *Art Nouveau 1900-1914,* Victoria & Albert Museum, London, 2000, New York section. (no. 19).
[inv.1999.33.16] 27

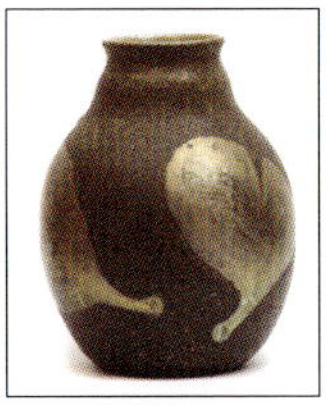

3 Cypriote Vase

Green glass with dark, pitted surface, three dark gold organic shapes and subtle iridescent finish. 28 cm.
Engraved: L.C.Tiffany. K1354 Favrile
[inv.1999.33.65] 113

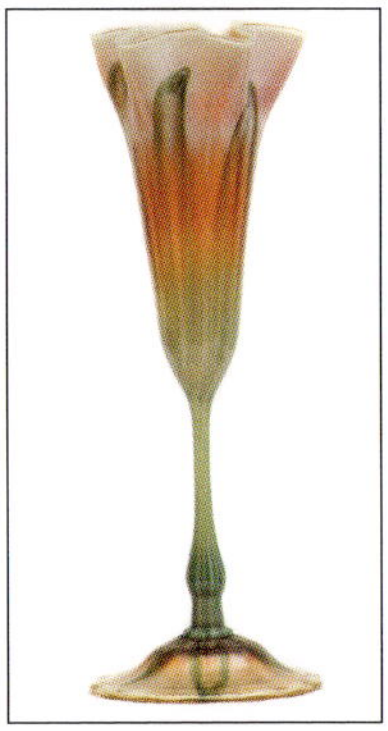

4 Flower Form Vase

Amber, gold, green, pink and white opalescent and translucent glass, the inside of the blossom with an orange lustre and 'onion skin' finish. 36. 8 cm.
Engraved: L.C.T.N4804
Bought from Lillian Nassau Gallery, New York, with grants from the Museums Libraries and Archives Council, the V&A Museum Purchase Grant Fund and the Art Fund, 2000.
Exhibited: *Northern Lights-100 Years of the National Art Collections Fund in the North West,* Harris Museum and Art Gallery, Preston, 2003.
118

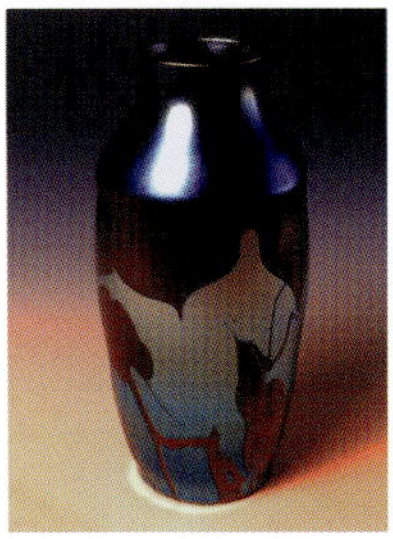

5 Blue Vase

Green glass with iridescent blue finish and dark silhouettes of leaves and fronds. 18 cm.
Engraved: L.C.Tiffany-Favrile N 7231
With original black and white LCT label.
Exhibited: Hamburg, 1999 (no. 146)
[inv.1999.33.63] 28

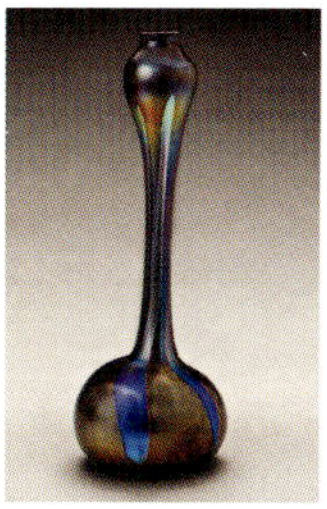

6 Onion Form Vase

Iridescent blue/black glass, with goose-neck and onion-shaped bowl, decorated with six brushed teardrop or leaf forms. 29.5 cm.
Engraved: L.C.Tiffany-Favrile N 7396
Exhibited: Hamburg, 1999 (no. 147); *Prelude: Cultural Influences in Art*, Cartwright Hall, Bradford, May 2006 - May 2011.
[inv.1999.33.11] 29

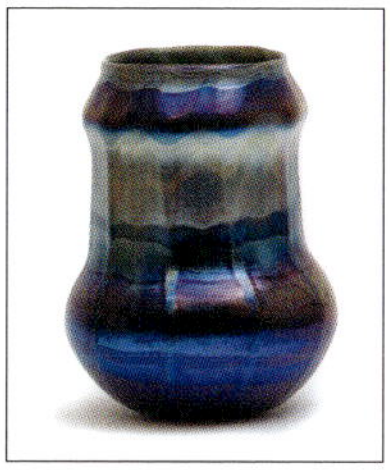

7 Blue Vase

Blown into a form to give a subtle, ten-sided shape, with vivid iridescent colour effects. One of over 10,000 vases produced as a special order, indicated by the 'o' prefix. 18 cm.
Engraved: o7201 L.C.T.
Bought from a private collection in Staffordshire, 2000.

92

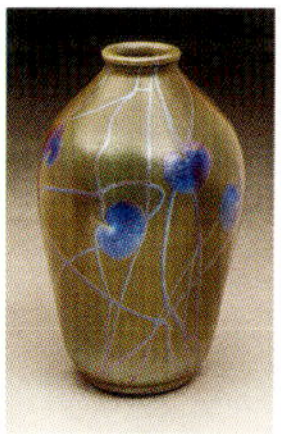

8 Green Vase

Botttle-shape, with iridescent finish and blue/purple Lily-pads and fronds. 18 cm.
Engraved: L.C.Tiffany-Q 9858-Favrile
With original black and white LCT label.
[inv.1999.33.5] 80

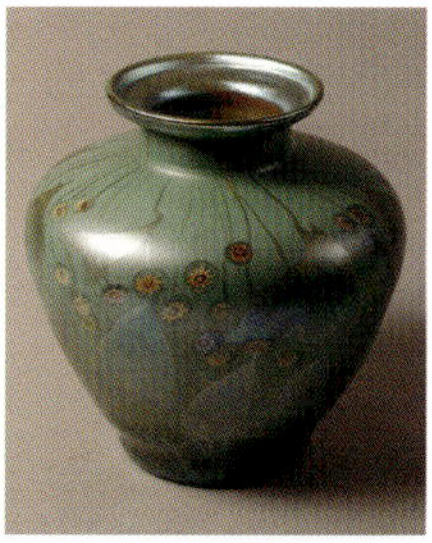

9 Millefiori Vase

Opaque silvery-green glass with strong, angular neck and iridescent finish, decorated with fronds, Lily-pads and 50 apricot-coloured flowers. 29.3 cm.
(*Millefiori:* meaning 1,000 flowers. Slivers were cut from a pre-formed cane of glass with the profile of a flower and adhered during the forming process. In this vase each flower has a 'halo' of the glass used to adhere it to the vase.)
Engraved: Louis C.Tiffany R4015
With original black and white LCT label.
Exhibited: Hamburg, 1999 (no. 155); *Art Nouveau 1900-1914*, Victoria & Albert Museum, London, 2000, New York section. (no. 18).
[inv.1999.33.10] 93

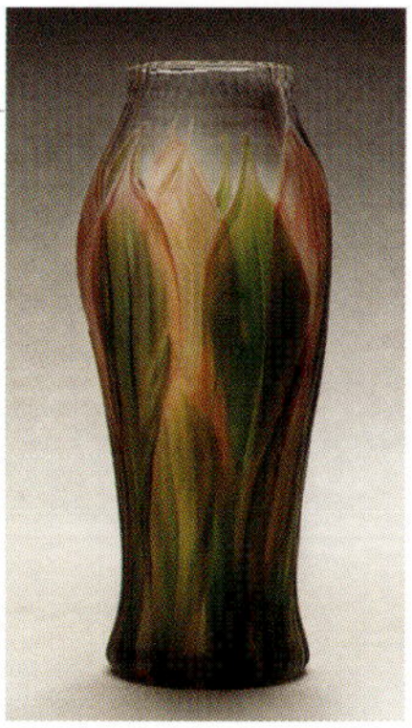

10 Cameo Vase

Layers of transparent, pink and green glass, blown into a mould to give a subtle, five-sided shape and cut to show 15 overlapping leaves and petals, the rim decorated with tiny cuts. 20.5 cm.
Engraved: W7842 L.C.Tiffany-Favrile
With original green/gold LCT label.
[inv.1999.33.29] 137

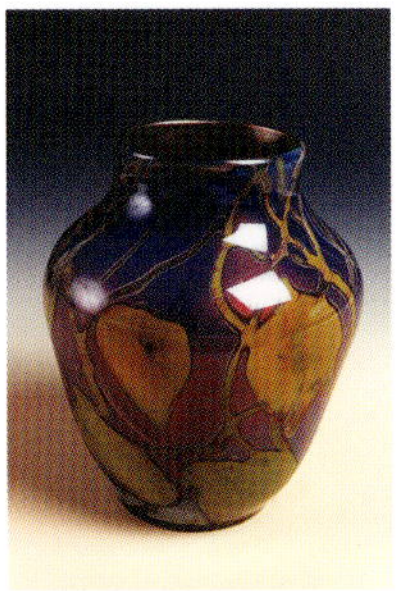

11 Paperweight Vase

In purple and blue reactive glass, lustred inside and decorated with lime green/mustard leaves, traditionally called an Autumn Leaf vase. 15 cm. (Paperweight: the final 'gather' of glass used was transparent, enhancing the colour and decoration of the vase. Reactive glass changes colour depending on whether it is exposed to direct or reflected light.)
Engraved: 297A L.C.Tiffany-Favrile
With original black and white LCT label.
Exhibited: Hamburg, 1999 (no. 160).
[inv.1999.33.30] 107

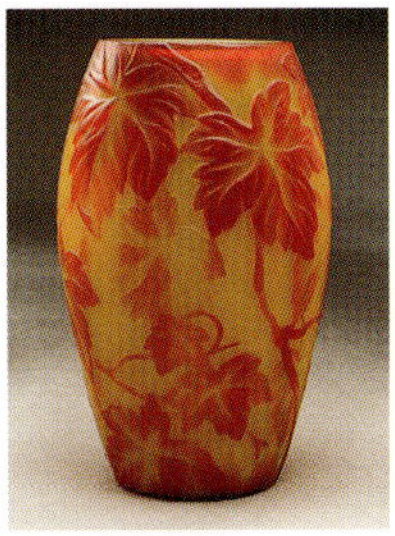

12 Cameo Vase

Layers of opaque yellow and red glass cut to show red foliage on yellow ground, lustred inside. 25 cm.
Engraved: L.C.Tiffany Favrile 9910A
With original black and white LCT label.
[inv.1999.33.2] 108

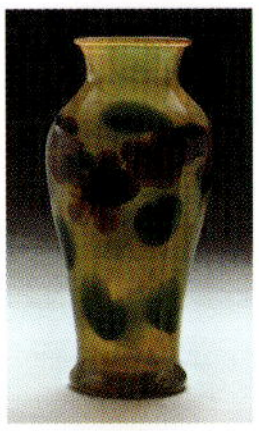

13 Millefiori Paperweight Vase

Cream/gold glass with internal orange lustre and decorated with leaves and seven brown flowers. 22.5 cm.
Engraved: L.C.Tiffany-Favrile 3327B
With original black and white LCT label.
[inv.1999.33.38] 56

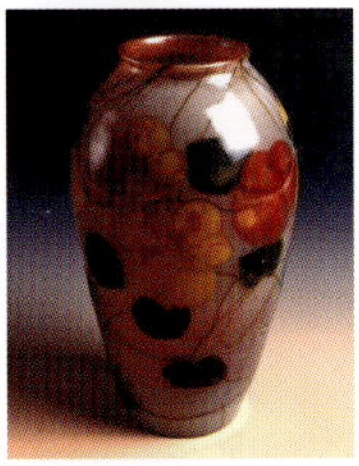

14 Millefiori Paperweight Vase

Pink opalescent glass with internal lustre, green leaves and eight yellow flowers. 21 cm.
Engraved: L.C.Tiffany 6662B-Favrile
With original green/gold LCT label.
Exhibited: Hamburg, 1999 (no. 165)
[inv.1999.33.20] 57

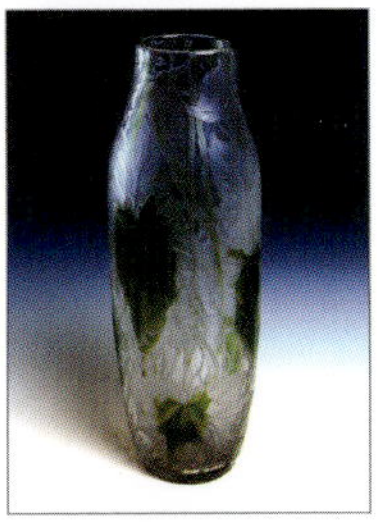

15 Intaglio Vase

Transluscent and green glass, bottle-shaped with vine-leaf decoration in ornate engraved lines, the leaves and fronds frosted. 31 cm.
Engraved: 7500 B. L.C.Tiffany Favrile
With original green/gold LCT label.
Exhibited: Hamburg, 1999 (no. 166)
[inv.1999.33.39] 81

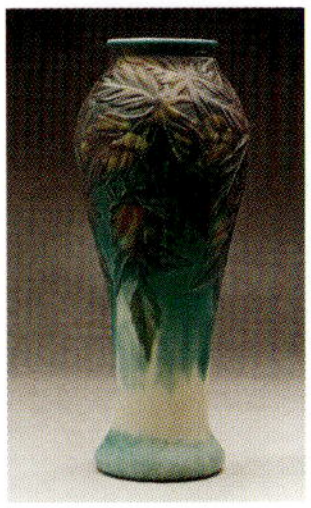

16 Cameo Vase

Opaque white and green layers with leaf decoration trailing to base of vase, lustred inside. 29 cm.
Engraved: 8798 B L.C.Tiffany. Favrile.
With original green/gold LCT label.
[inv.1999.33.4] 69

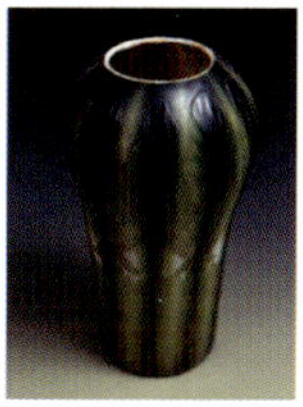

17 **Cameo Vase**

Opaque white and green layers of glass with ten overlapping leaves and subtle iridescence at the base. 22 cm.
Engraved: 471C L.C.Tiffany-Favrile
With original black and white LCT label.
58

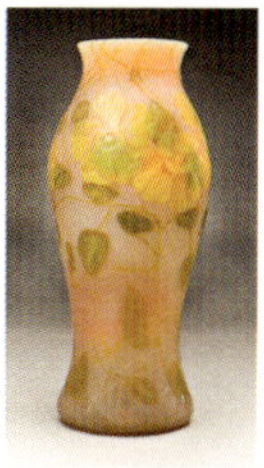

18 **Cameo Vase**

Opaque yellow, green and pink layers with green leaves and yellow flowers and internal lustre. 30 cm.
Engraved: 1747C L.C.Tiffany-Favrile
[inv.1999.33.3] 136

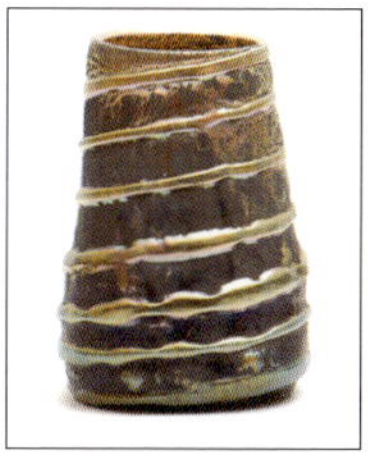

19 **Lava Vase**

Brown glass in unsophisticated, basic shape with subtle iridescence and spiral of gold 'lava' falling from the neck to the base around sooty body. 22 cm.
Engraved: 2579C. L. C.Tiffany-Favrile
With paper label: PGM
Exhibited: Hamburg, 1999 (no. 169); *Art Nouveau 1900-1914*,
Victoria & Albert Museum, London, 2000,
New York section. (no. 20).
[inv.1999.33.74] 114

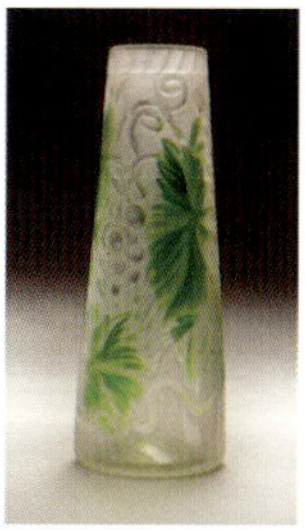

20 **Intaglio Vase**

Translucent glass with green leaves, grapevine decoration and a rope motif around the neck. 30 cm.
Engraved: 3076C L.C.Tiffany-Favrile MO97
With original black and white LCT label.
[inv.1999.33.42] 59

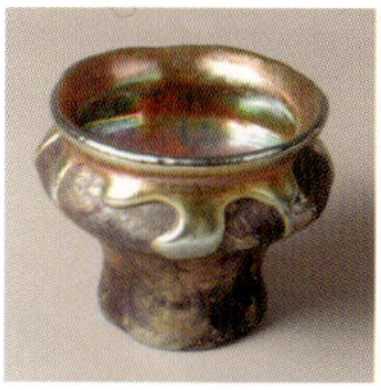

21 **Lava Vase**

Brown glass in simple shape with pitted sooty surface and rich iridescent effects, with gold 'lava' dropping from the wide rim. 10.5 cm.
Engraved: 3744C L.C.Tiffany-Favrile
[inv.1999.33.77] 143

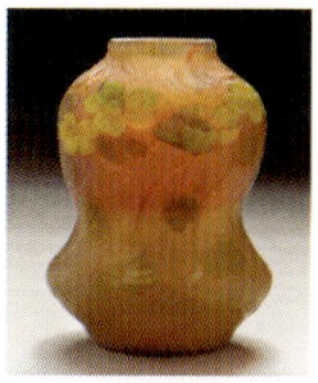

22 **Cameo Vase**

Double-gourd shape in opaque pink glass, yellow flowers and green leaves and internal orange lustre. 16.5 cm.
Engraved: 5012C L.C.Tiffany-Favrile
With original green/gold LCT label.
[inv.1999.33.1] 70

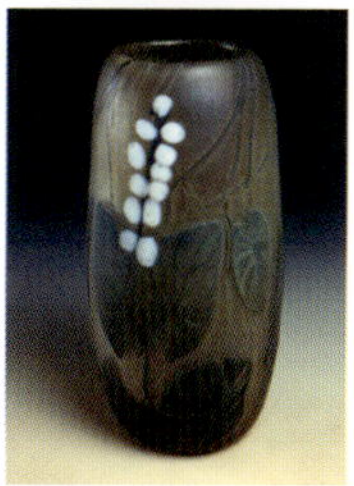

23 **Cameo Vase**

Layers of green and opalescent white glass, with internal lustre, Water-lily leaves and trails and three Lily-of-the-Valley flowers. 24.5 cm.
Engraved: 5015C L.C.Tiffany-Favrile
With original green/gold LCT label.
Exhibited: Hamburg, 1999 (no. 171)
[inv.1999.33.36] 82

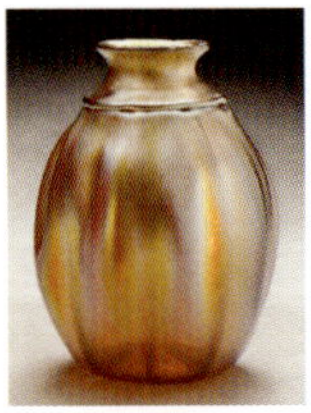

24 Gold Vase

Seed-pod form, with iridescent lustre, the neck made separately. 16 cm.
Engraved: 9916C L.C.Tiffany-Favrile
With original black and white LCT label.
[inv.1999.33.81] 134

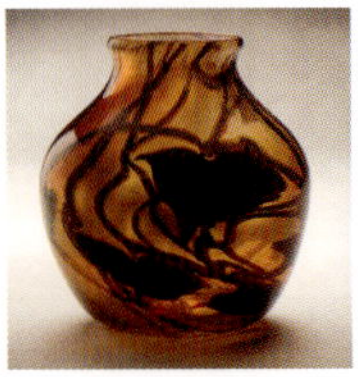

25 Paperweight Vase

In russet and gold glass, lustred inside and with leaves and fronds. 12 cm.
Engraved: 9916C L.C.Tiffany-Favrile Y6694
With original black and white LCT label.
[inv.1999.33.27] 141

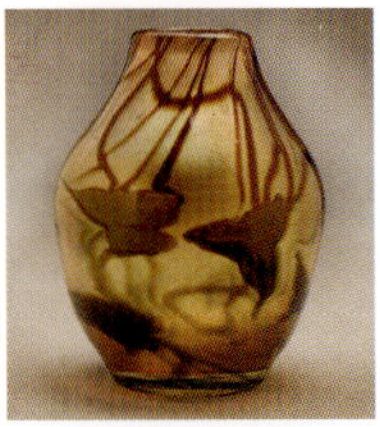

26 Paperweight Vase

In fawn and pink glass, lustred inside and with lime-green leaves and fronds. 13.5 cm.
Engraved: 9925C L.C.Tiffany
With original black and white LCT label.
[inv.1999.33.17] 109

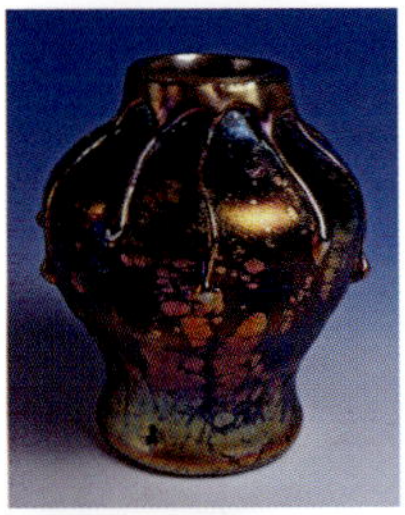

27 Lava Vase

Brown glass in uneven rounded shape, with glimmering rainbow iridescence and nine elegant gold 'lava' droplets spilling over the neck and down the pitted sooty body. 15.3 cm.
Engraved: 9926C L.C.Tiffany-Favrile
Exhibited: Hamburg, 1999 (no. 172); *Art Nouveau 1900-1914*, Victoria & Albert Museum, London, 2000, New York section. (no. 21).
[inv.1999.33.82] 114

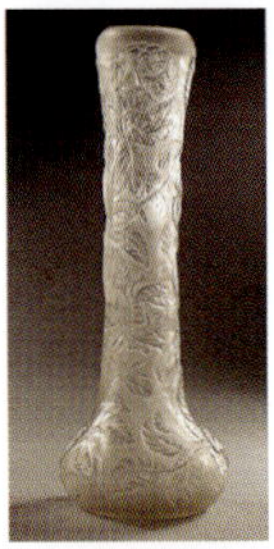

28 Rose Vase

Intaglio rock-crystal glass, slightly lustred inside with bulbous base, frosted matt surface and polished decoration, with representations of eight Roses in bud, open and full-blown states. 51 cm.
Engraved: 232D L.C.Tiffany-Favrile
[inv.1999.33.37] 62

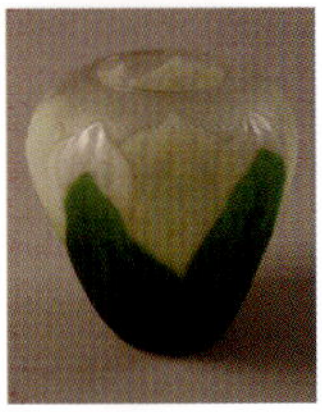

29 Cameo Vase

Opaque, green and white glass with Water-lily decoration. 13 cm.
Engraved: L.C.Tiffany-Favrile/233D
With original black and white LCT label.
[inv.1999.33.33] 60

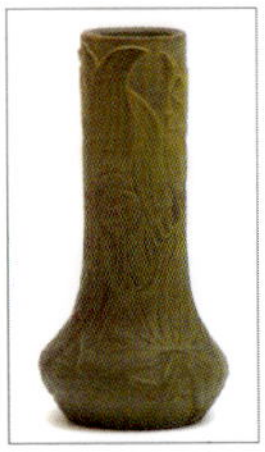

30 Intaglio Vase

Opaque green glass, decorated with representations of Water-lily leaves, seed-heads and flowers. 24 cm.
Engraved: L.C.Tiffany-Favrile 279D
[inv.1999.33.9] 30

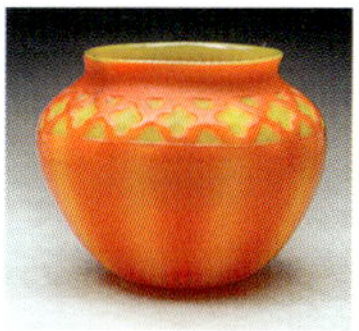

31 Cameo Bowl

Opaque yellow and orange glass with lattice-work decoration and subtle striped effect. 7 cm.
Engraved: L. C.Tiffany-Favrile 4121D
[inv. 1999.33.35] 34

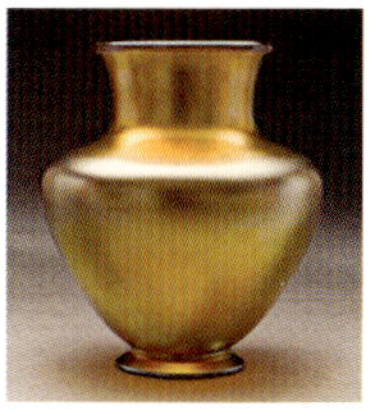

32 Gold Vase

Iridescent glass in pyriform shape. 27 cm.
Engraved: 52E L.C.Tiffany. Favrile
With original black and white LCT label
[inv.1999.33.14] 116

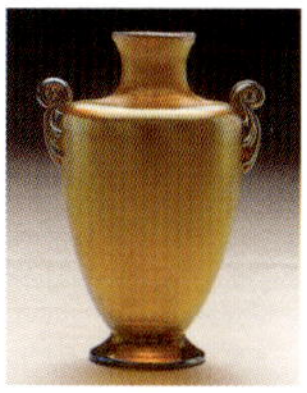

33 Gold Vase

Iridescent glass in urn shape with scroll handles. 16 cm.
Engraved: L.C.Tiffany. Favrile 5011E
[inv.1999.33.69] 117

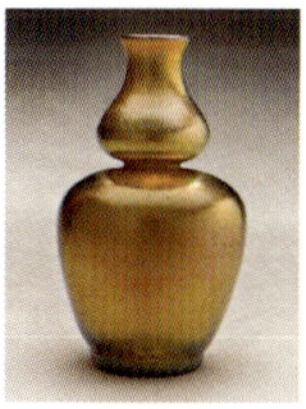

34 Gold Vase

Iridescent glass in double-gourd shape.16.5 cm.
Engraved: 5012E L.C.Tiffany-Favrile
With original black and white LCT label.
[inv.1999.33.72] 136

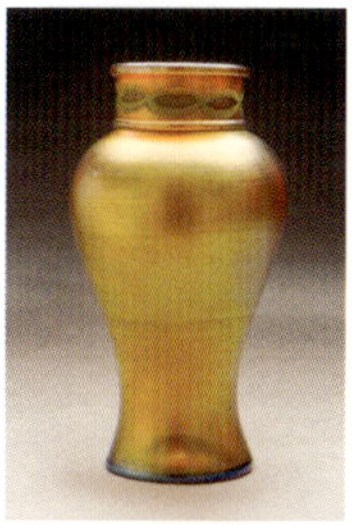

35 Gold Tel El Amarna Vase

Iridescent glass with yellow *guilloche* decoration at neck. 22.5 cm. (*guilloche:* ancient repetitive decoration of two ribbons winding around a series of regularly spaced points). See cat. no. 39 for Tel El Amarna decoration.
Engraved: L.C.Tiffany-Favrile 5013E
With original black and white LCT label.
[inv.1999.33.70] 51

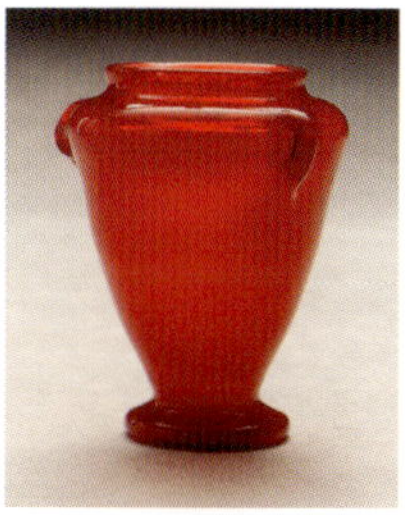

36 Samian Red Vase

Miniature cabinet piece with three loop handles and paperweight finish. 8.5 cm.
Engraved: L.C.Tiffany-Favrile 5015E
With original black and white LCT label.
Exhibited: Hamburg, 1999 (no. 175)
[inv.1999.33.15] 52

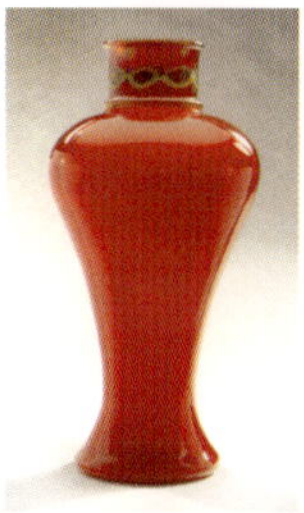

37 Samian Red Vase

With paperweight finish and guilloche decoration in yellow. 27 cm.
Engraved: 5018E L.CTiffany-Favrile.
With original black and white LCT label.
Exhibited: Hamburg, 1999 (no. 176)
[inv.1999.33.6] 53

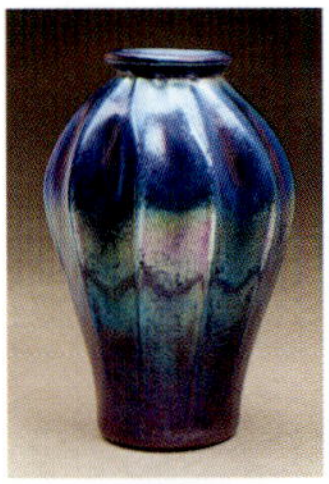

38 Blue Vase

Iridescent glass, blown into a form to achieve seed-pod shape. 16.3 cm.
Engraved: L.C.Tiffany-Favrile 5019E
With original black and white LCT label.
[inv.1999.33.12] 94

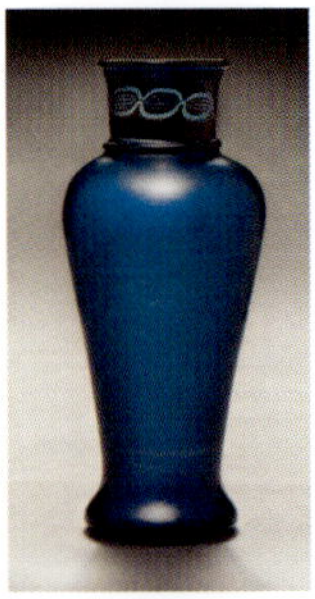

39 Blue Tel El Amarna Vase

Neck with pale blue *guilloche* decoration. 18 cm.
The colours and decoration of Tel El Amarna vases were inspired by a visit Tiffany made in 1878 to the excavated tomb of the 14th-century Pharaoh, Akenaten. The blue of these vases, called Mazarin, was developed to evoke the turquoise glazes of the pottery found there.
Engraved: 5021E L.C.Tiffany-Favrile.
With original black and white LCT label.
[inv.1999.33.71] 54

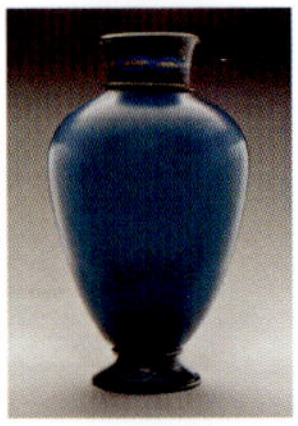

40 Blue Tel El Amarna Vase

Neck and foot with pale blue *guilloche* decoration. 38 cm.
Engraved: 5022E L. C.Tiffany-Favrile.
[inv.1999.33.68] 144

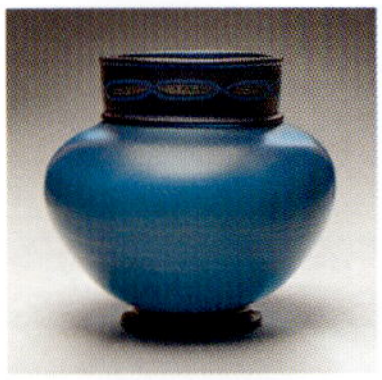

41 Blue Tel El Amarna Vase

Rounded shape, neck with pale blue *guilloche* decoration. 13 cm.
Engraved: 5024E L.C.Tiffany-Favrile.
With original black and white LCT label.
[inv.1999.33.79] 55

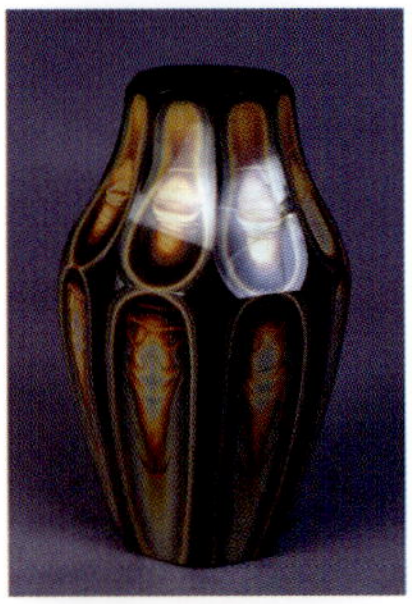

42 Agate Vase

Cut with eight facets to reveal eight thin layers of glass. 19 cm.
Agate glass was designed to look like semi-precious stones such as Chalcedony or Jasper. Originally made in 1st century BC Rome, Renaissance glass-makers revived it but it is a rare glass because it is difficult to make successfully. This is a spectacular example of the type. A similar vase in a jewelled, bronze mount is in the Anchorman Collection in Nagoya, Japan.
Engraved: L.C.Tiffany-Favrile 5025E
With original black and white LCT label.
Exhibited: Hamburg, 1999 (no. 177).
[inv.1999.33.19] 83

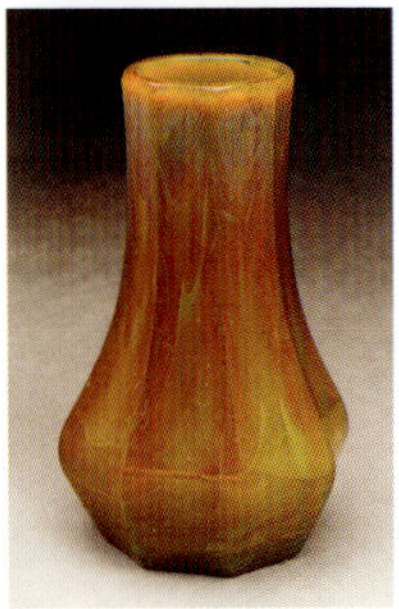

43 Marbleised Vase

Yellow ochre glass with 'vein' effects, cut with eight facets. 15.5 cm.
Engraved: 5026E [remainder illegible]
With original black and white LCT label.
[inv.1999.33.18] 84

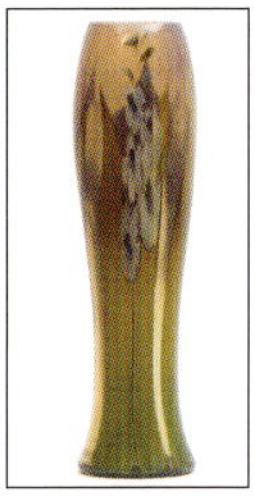

44 Gladiola Vase

Millefiori paperweight glass in lime-green and mauve, with internal lustre, tall, elegant leaves and a white Gladiola flower with ten blooms. 42.5 cm.
Engraved: 5027E L.C.Tiffany. Favrile
[inv.1999.33.43] 66

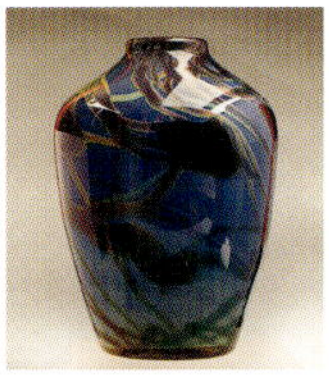

45 Paperweight Vase

In bottle-shape, blue/green reactive glass decorated with Lily-pads and trails. Reactive glass changes colour depending on whether it is exposed to direct or reflected light. 14.5 cm.
Engraved: 5029E L.C.Tiffany-Favrile.
With original black and white LCT label.
[inv.1999.33.13] 95

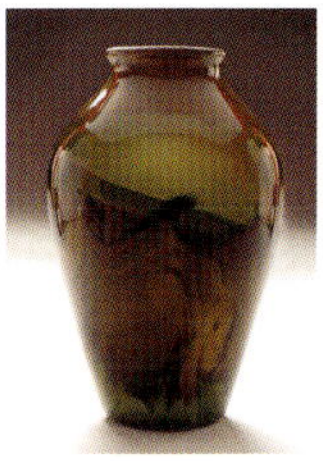

46 Paperweight Vase

Marbleised glass, lustred inside, with green and brown swirling decoration (with a modern hole in the base). 21 cm.
Engraved: L.C.Tiffany-Favrile 5032E
[inv.1999.33.22] 85

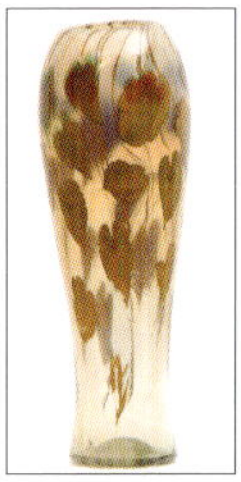

47 Paperweight Vase

Monumental translucent and iridescent glass, with 18 green/orange and lime leaves, some with 'halo' effect, and fronds trailing downwards to base. 42.5 cm.
Engraved: 5033E L.C.Tiffany-Favrile.
With remnant of original LCT Label.
[inv.1999.33.40] 120

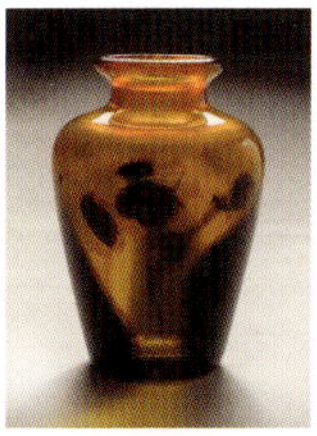

48 Millefiori Paperweight Vase

Lustred inside, with large green leaves and small brown and cream flowers. 15 cm.
Engraved: 5035E L. C.Tiffany-Favrile
With original black and white LCT label.
[inv. 1999.33.26] 138

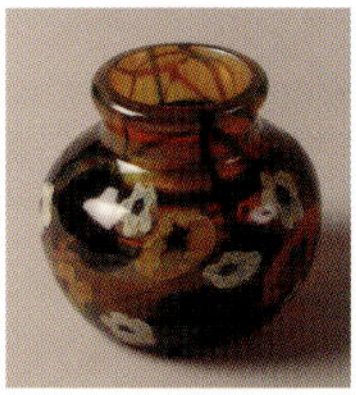

49 Millefiori Paperweight Vase

Orange glass, lustred inside, with 15 white and beige Morning Glory flowers and green and brown leaves and fronds. 11.5 cm.
Engraved: 5036E L.C.Tiffany-Favrile
With original black and white LCT label.
[inv.1999.33.24] 110

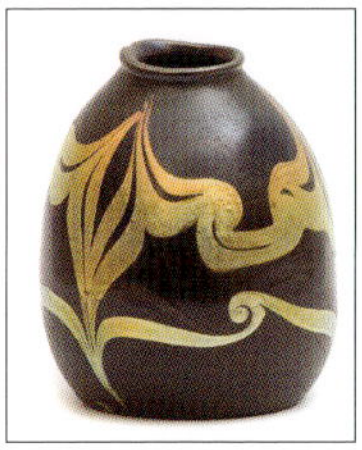

50 Black Vase

Blown into irregular, gourd-like form, with free-flowing gold patterns and subtle iridescence. 16 cm.
Engraved: 5037 E L.C.Tiffany - Favrile
With original black and white LCT label.
[inv.1999.33.76] 31

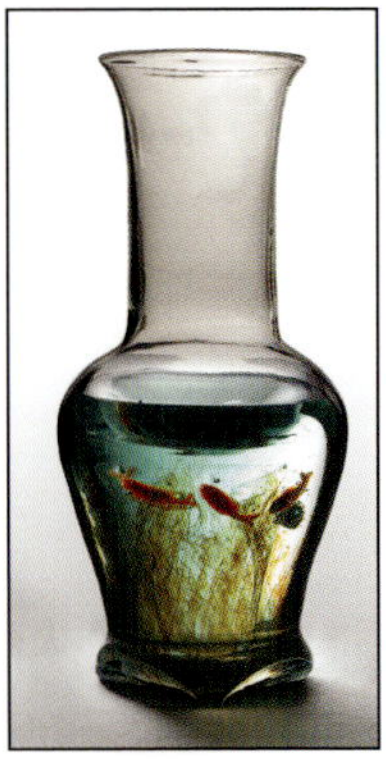

51 Aquamarine Vase

Transparent glass decorated with six goldfish, pond-weed and air bubbles encased in sea-green glass to represent water. 37.5 cm.
This spectacular example of the Tiffany paperweight technique is very rare and dates to late 1913. It was made by Arthur Saunders who was sent by Tiffany to Bermuda to study marine life in a glass-bottomed boat in preparation. A similar Aquamarine but with a longer neck appeared on the U.S. market recently.
Engraved: 1999H L. C. Tiffany
Exhibited: Hamburg, 1999 (no. 179)
[inv.1999.33.23] 119

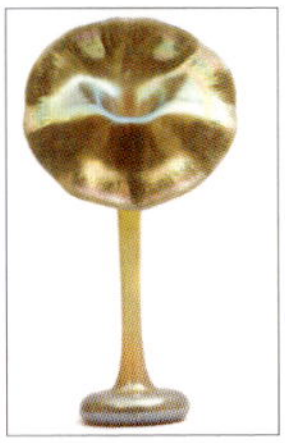

52 Jack-in-the-Pulpit Vase

Gold Flower form, hollow throughout with slender stem, circular blossom, spectacular iridescent colours and 'onion-skin' finish. 47.5 cm.
Engraved: 6365H L.C.Tiffany. Favrile
Given by Mr Joseph Marshall of Blackburn in 1967.
[inv.1999.33.73] 121

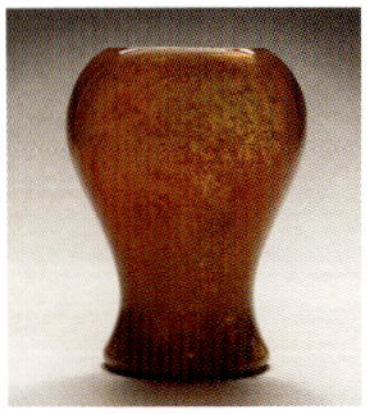

53 Paperweight Vase

In classical Chinese shape, orange with mottled mustard yellow decoration. 15 cm.
Engraved: 1588J. L.C.Tiffany-Favrile
With original green/gold LCT label.
[inv.1999.33.21] 142

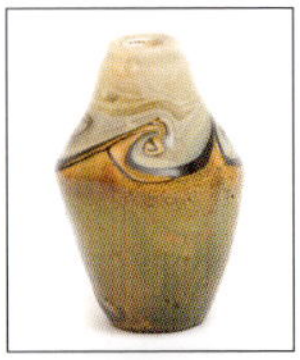

54 Miniature Paperweight Vase

Marbleised glass cabinet piece in mustard, lime-green and cream with dark, swirling line. 10 cm.
Engraved: 6415J L.C.Tiffany Favrile
[inv.1999.33.28] 128

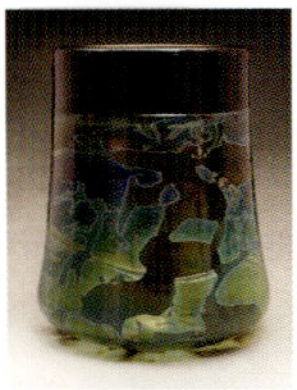

55 Paperweight Vase

Green/blue glass with silver inclusions, the neck made separately. 13 cm.
Engraved: 1139L Exhibition Piece L.C.Tiffany-Favrile.
[inv.1999.33.7] 96

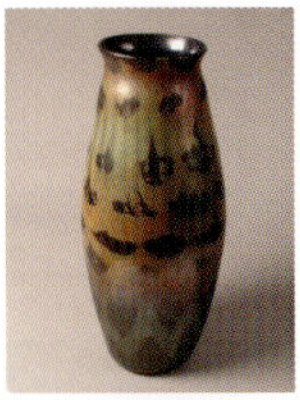

56 Cypriote Vase

Monumental vase with gold to brown/black finish, decorated with broad brush-stroke patterns, the whole with unusual skin-like texture and subtle pink to blue surface iridescence. 65 cm.
Engraved: 507N Louis C.Tiffany
[inv.1999.33.41] 129

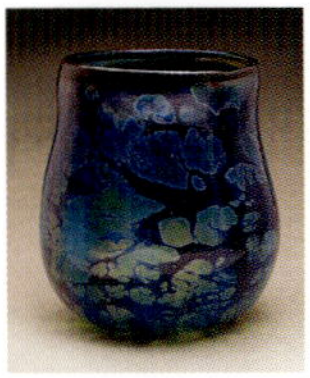

57 Paperweight Vase

Blue/green glass with silver inclusions. 9.8 cm.
Engraved: X1343N Louis C.Tiffany-Favrile/special exhibition
With original green/gold LCT label.
[inv.1999.33.67] 97

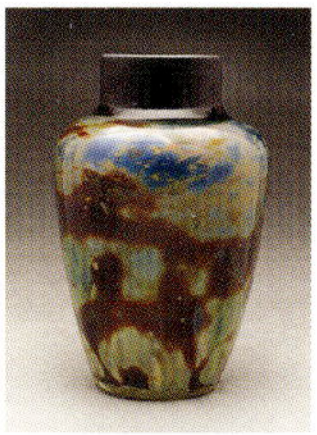

58 Paperweight Vase

Blue, brown and green glass with silver/gold inclusions, slightly ribbed towards the base, the neck made separately. 15 cm.
Engraved: 3605N L. C. Tiffany Inc Favrile
[inv.1999.33.8] 111

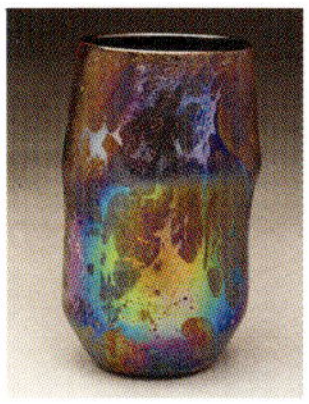

59 Cypriote Vase

Irregular, beaker form with vibrant iridescent colour effects. 14 cm.
Engraved: L.C.T. Favrile 5355N.
[inv.1999.33.64] 65

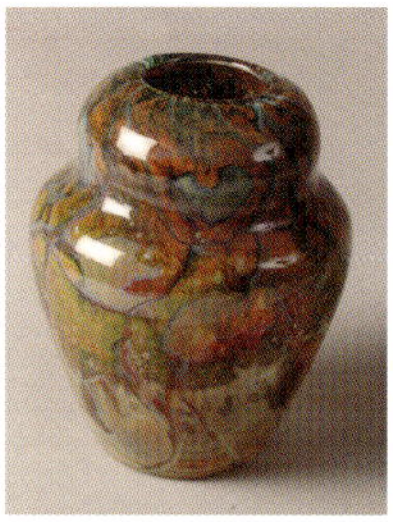

60 Paperweight Vase

Double-gourd shape in transparent and multi-coloured glass, decorated with air-bubbles. 13 cm.
Engraved: 3286P L.C Tiffany-Favrile.
With original green/gold LCT label and $40 price label.
[inv.1999.33.25] 112

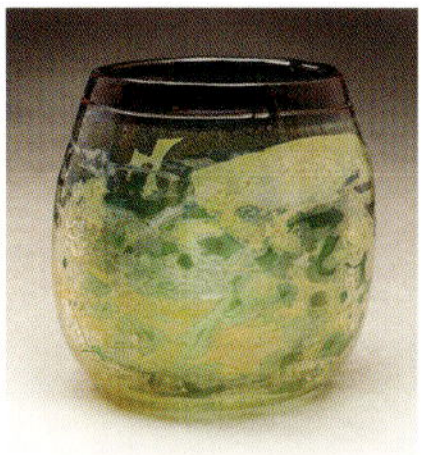

61 Paperweight Vase

Round green glass, with gold inclusions, neck made separately. 9.8 cm.
Engraved: 3309P L.C.Tiffany Favrile.
With original green/gold LCT label.
[inv.1999.33.66] 98

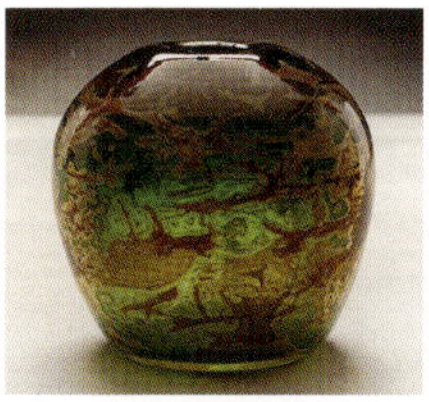

62 Paperweight Vase

In green glass with gold inclusions. 8.5 cm.
Engraved: 3317P L.C.Tiffany.
With original green/gold LCT label.
[inv.1999.33.31] 99

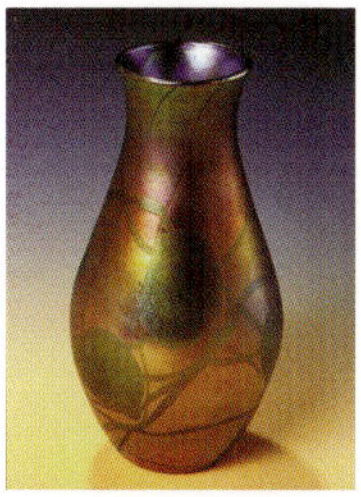

63 Gold Vase

Lustred inside, with green/blue Lily-pads, trails and rainbow colour effects. 23.2 cm.
Engraved: 3318P Louis C.Tiffany-Inc. Favrile
With original green/gold LCT label and $25 price label.
[inv.1999.33.78] 86

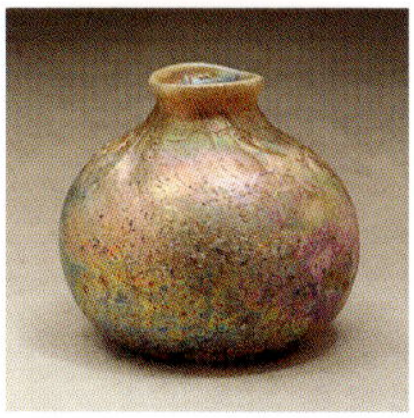

64 Cypriote Vase

Classical round shape with pitted surface and subtle iridescence. 7 cm.
Engraved: L.C.T. Favrile 3320P
With original green/gold LCT label.
[inv.1999.33.62] 63

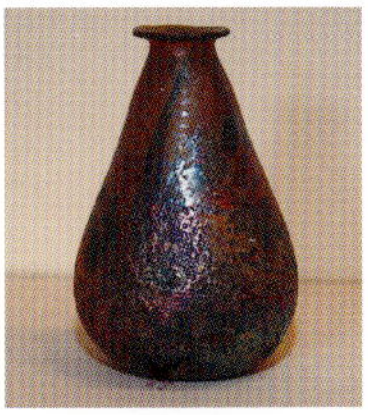

65 Cypriote Vase

Classical flask shape with pitted surface
and subtle iridescence. 9 cm.
Engraved: 3321P
[inv.1999.33.61] 130

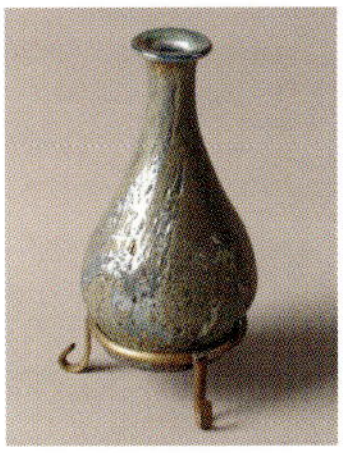

66 Cypriote Vase with brass stand

Classical round-bottomed flask shape with
pitted surface and subtle iridescence, the stand
like those used in museums to support antique
round-bottomed flasks. 12 cm.
Engraved: L.C.T.Favrile 3323P
[inv.1999.33.60] 64

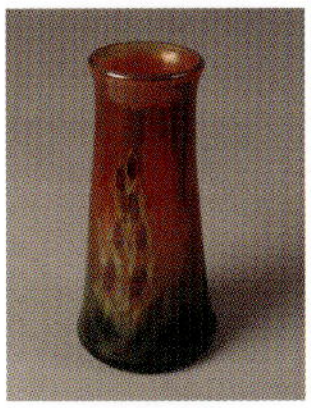

67 Millefiori Paperweight Vase

Internal lustre with green leaves at base and three Gladiola flowers,
each with seven blooms. 21 cm.
Engraved: 3562P L.C.Tiffany-Favrile
With original black and white LCT label.
[inv.1999.33.32] 61

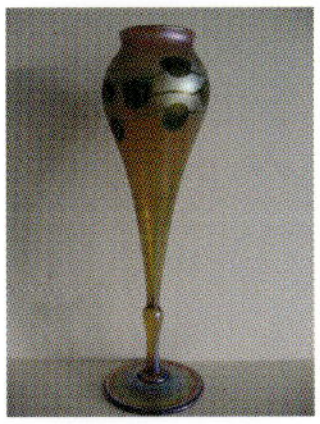

68 Gold Stem Vase

Lustred inside, with green Philodendron leaves
bound with fronds. 30.8 cm.
Engraved: 3766P-1517. L.C.Tiffany-Favrile.
With original $25 price label.
[inv.1999.33.80] 87

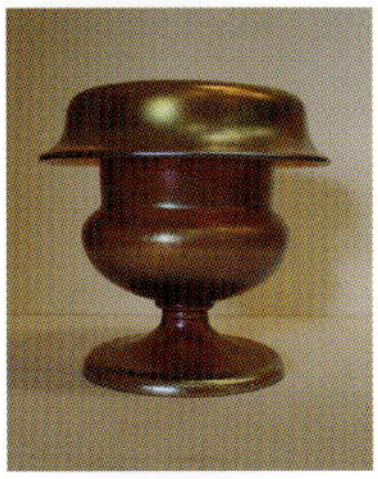

69 Gold Vase

With bulbous turnover rim, originally ascribed to Tiffany, now ascribed to
Johann Lötz Witwe of Klostermühle, Bohemia. 18.5 cm.
Engraved: D9349 L.C.Tiffany-Favrile.
Bought with the aid of grants from the Museums Libraries
and Archives Council and the V&A Museum
Purchase Grant Fund, around 1980.
123

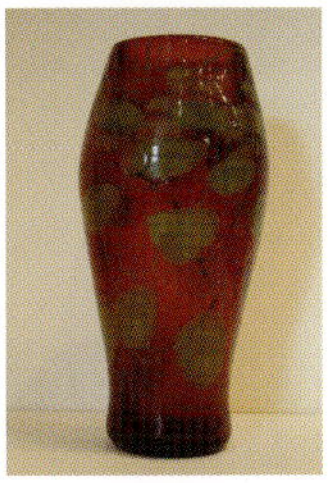

70 Paperweight Vase

Red glass decorated with green leaves and fronds. 23 cm.
Engraved: 9197A L.C.Tiffany-Favrile
Broken during a burglary in September 1993. Not on display.

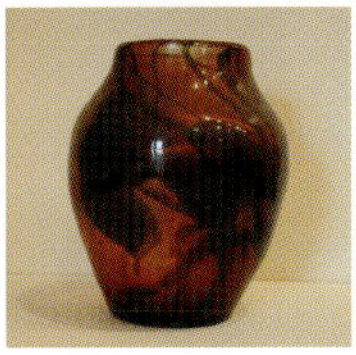

71 Paperweight Vase

Decorated with blue/brown/mauve swirling forms. 18 cm.
Engraved: 9190 L.C.Tiffany - Favrile
Broken during a burglary in September 1993. Not on display.

Mosaics and Related Drawings

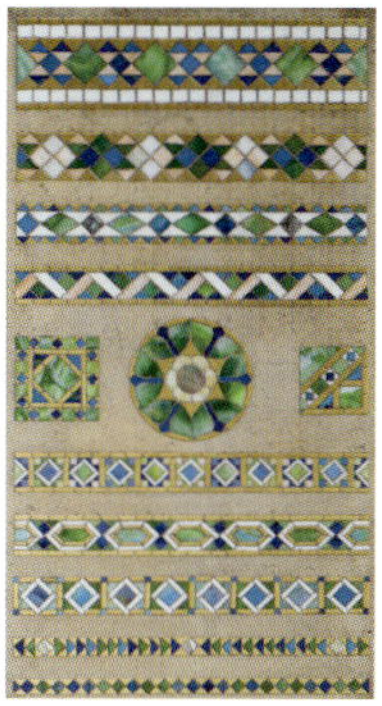

72 Mosaic Sampler for Citizens' Savings Bank, Cleveland, Ohio, USA

Composed of *Favrile* glass tesserae in blues, greens, gold and marbleised glass, in *cosmati* style. 72 x 38 cm.

This sampler probably relates to an unsuccessful tender, of around 1890, to decorate the Bank with murals by Walter Crane (1845-1915). Similar designs were provided for the Chicago Public Library, (now Chicago Cultural Centre), under the direction of Jacob Holzer (1858-1938), head of the mosaics shop until 1896. *Cosmati* style derives from Roman church floors of the 1200s. See *The Mosaics of Louis Comfort Tiffany* by Edith Crouch, p.169.

67

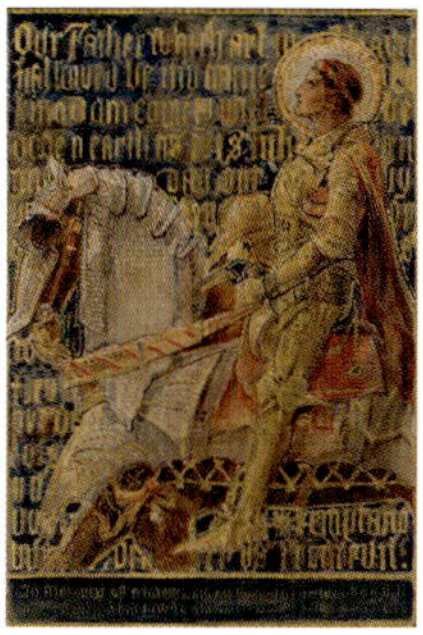

73 Composition sketch for a memorial to an unknown person

First idea in water-colour, ink and gouache for a memorial depicting St George in front of the Lord's Prayer, said to be for the First Presbyterian Church, Binghampton, New York State, USA.

Unsigned, formerly thought to be by Joseph Briggs, now ascribed to Frederick Wilson (1858-1932). 21.5 x 14.5 cm.

This drawing relates to cat. no. 74 and to a design by Wilson for a memorial tablet for Ernest Whitehouse, killed in the South African war in 1896. See Crouch, p.106. See also cat. no. 144 below.

23

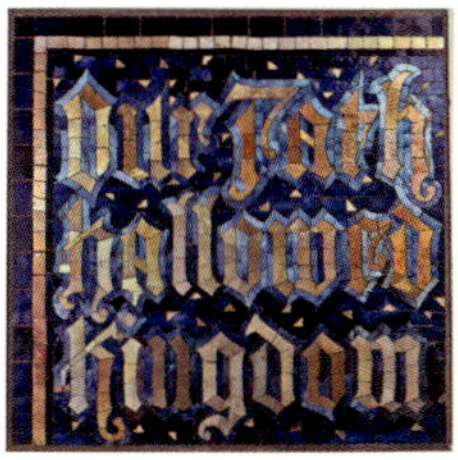

74 Mosaic Sampler for a memorial to an unknown person

Composed of *Favrile* glass tessarae in blue and gold, showing the top left-hand section of a memorial, as described in catalogue number 73. The words 'Our Fath/Hallowed/Kingdom' from the Lord's Prayer, are defined in gothic script. 41 x 41 cm.

Illustrated in Crouch, p.49. See also cat. no. 144 below.

24

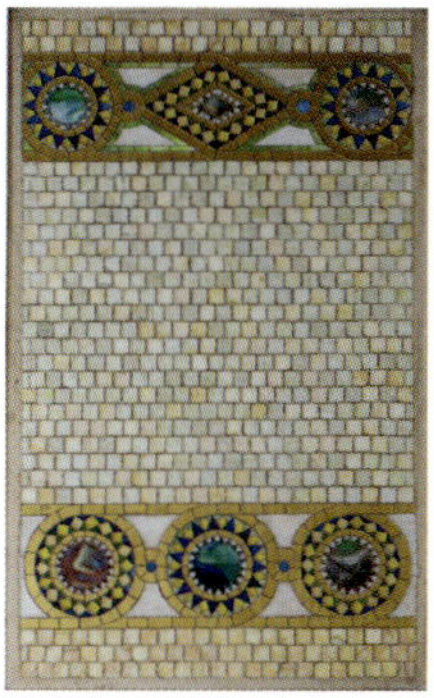

75 Mosaic Sampler for First National Bank, Pittsburg, Pennsylvania, USA

Composed of *Favrile* glass tessarae in white, cream, green, blue, yellow and transparent glass over gold leaf, with roundels of marbleised green glass. 72 x 44 cm.

This sample relates to the new bank of 1898. Tiffany personally supervised the installation of the Vermont marble, mosaic and mother-of-pearl interiors of the banking rooms. The *Pittsburg Post* noted at the time that it was fortunate that the interiors could be cleaned with a 'wet sponge or a hose,' given the industrial pollution in the city. The bank was demolished in 1908 and a second bank opened in 1909. Illustrated in Crouch, p.169.

68

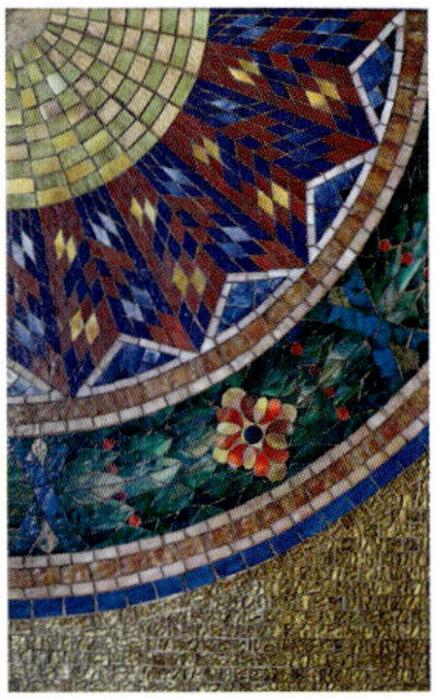

76 Mosaic Sampler for the Philadelphia Mint.

Composed of *Favrile* glass tesserae in red, green and gold, with mother-of-pearl. 83 x 52 cm.
The Philadelphia Mint building was completed in 1901. Tiffany Studios adapted compositions for mosaics discovered in Pompei in 1895 for the seven wall mosaics of this scheme which feature children using ancient handmade methods to make coins. They are now at the new Philadelphia Mint. The Haworth sampler relates to the floor mosaic, which remains in what is now a Community College. Briggs probably worked on this commission for Tiffany in the mosaics shop. Exhibited: Hamburg, 1999 (no. 12). Illustrated in Crouch, p. 229.
[inv.1999.33.55] 127

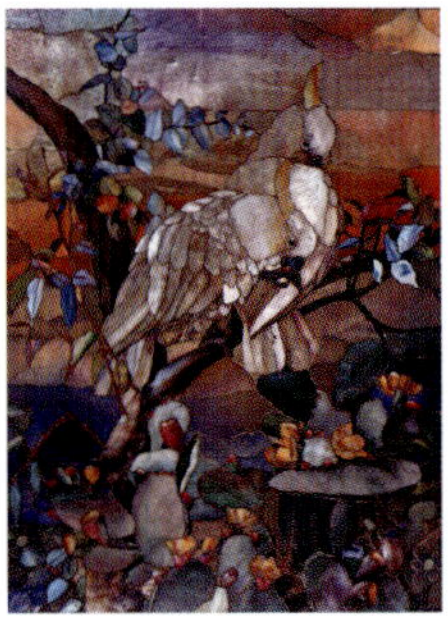

77 Mosaic Panel with Sulphur-Crested Cockatoos

Attributed to Joseph Briggs, around 1908.
Composed of multi-coloured, iridescent *Favrile* glass tesserae, laid into a narrow bronze tray with hanging devices on the reverse. 8.5 x 59 x 2 cm.
This is one of Tiffany Studios' most remarkable glass mosaic works. It depicts a pair of Greater Sulphur-Crested Cockatoos, native to Australia and New Guinea, perched in a tree against a sunset sky. It was almost certainly made by Briggs and demonstrates the full creativity of Tiffany's glassmakers. Instead of being cut in traditional squares, the tesserae follow the organic forms of the representation. Fore-runners of this type of mosaic can be found in 18th century Florentine furniture and the composition may have a Japanese source.
Exhibitions: *The Alaska-Yukon-Pacific Exposition,* Seattle, USA, 1909; *Masterworks of Louis Comfort Tiffany,* Tokyo, 1991 (no. 89); Hamburg, 1999 (no. 14); *Art Nouveau 1900-1914,* Victoria & Albert Museum, London, 2000, New York section (no. 22) (detail reproduced as frontispiece); *Louis Comfort Tiffany-Artist for the Ages,* Seattle, Toledo, Dallas, and Pittsburg, 2005/6 (no. 70); *Tiffany Glass, A Passion for Colour,* Paris, Montreal and Richmond, Virginia, 2009/10 (no. 152).
[inv.1999.33.59] 106

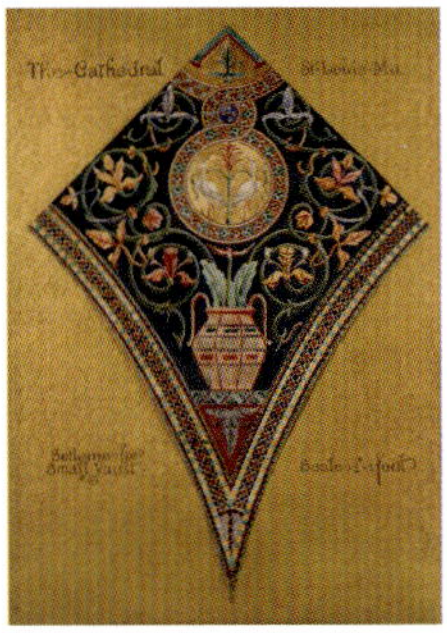

78 Six designs for St Louis Cathedral, Missouri, USA

Water-colour and ink on paper mounted on gold card.
Each design 27.5 x 19.7 cm.
These designs, nos.1,2,5,6,7 and 8 of the complete set of eight, relate to the decorations of the ceiling of the Chapel of the Blessed Virgin in St Louis Catherdral. The Chapel was decorated by Tiffany Studios from 1912 to 1914.
Each inscribed: The Cathedral / St.Louis. Mo./.scheme.for small vault / scale 1"= 1foot (and each signed on mount): Joseph Briggs.
25

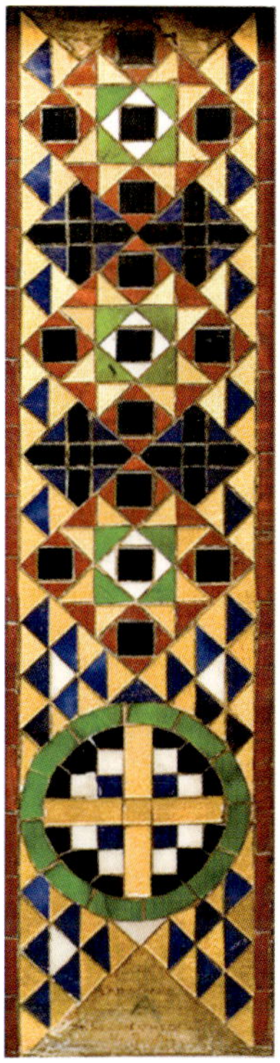

79 Mosaic Sampler for St Louis Cathedral

Composed of *Favrile* glass tesserae in maroon, black, green, white, blue and clear glass on gold background. 51 x 13 cm.
St Louis Cathedral, decorated with 41.5 million tesserae between 1912 and 1988, is the largest such decorated interior in the world.
Tiffany Studios were involved only with the Lady Chapel, for which this relates to the wall decoration.
Inscribed: LADY.CHAPEL /A/ ST.LOUIS CATHEDRAL/ U.S.A
26

80 Sampler for a Reredos in Christ Episcopal Church, Brooklyn, New York, USA

Composite in the place of marble, inlaid with mother-of-pearl. 46 x 46 cm.
This design shows the influence of the abstract arabesques of Islamic art and was made around 1915. Tiffany Studios decorated many churches across the USA with stained glass windows. Here, chancel, altar, reredos, pulpit, lectern and railings as well as windows were provided. One of Tiffany's last commissions, the Church was completely renovated and decorated in 1916. It was awarded 'Landmark' status by the New York Landmarks Commission in 1969.
50

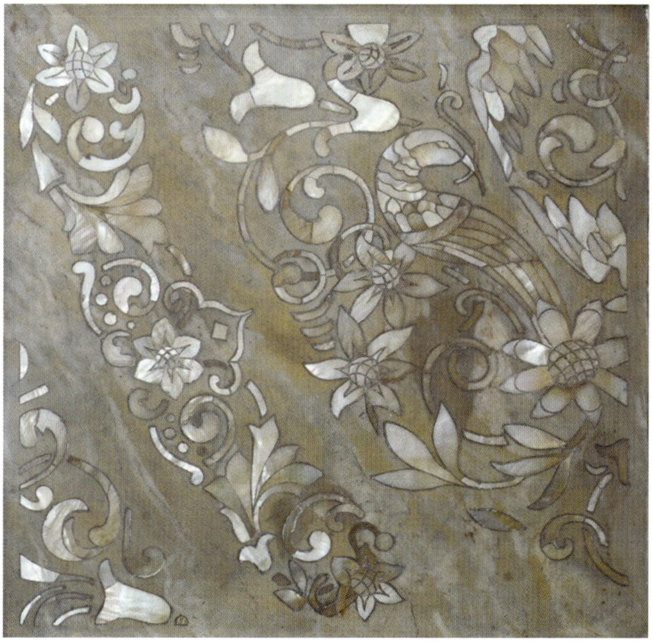

Other Tiffany Studios Products

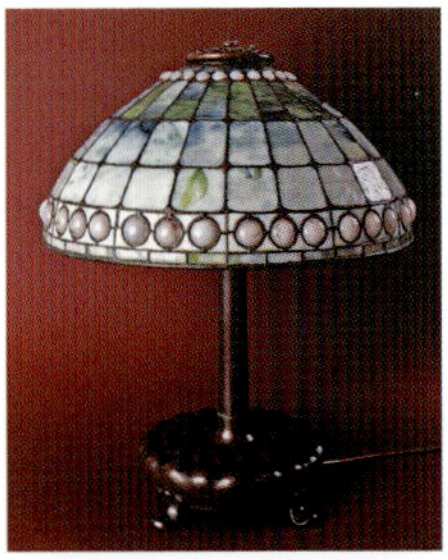

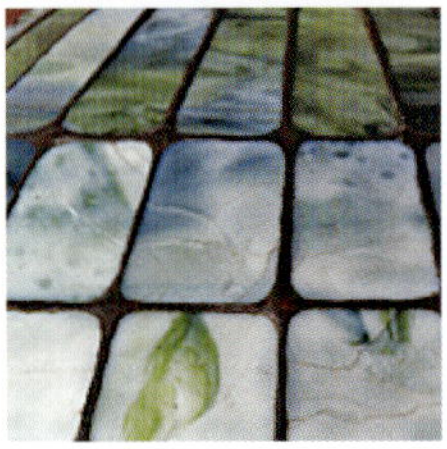

81 Tiffany Lamp

Cast bronze base, with electric light fittings, bronze finial and leaded glass Mushroom-shaped shade in green and white marbleised glass, edged with opalescent jewels. Made around 1900. 50 cm.
Inscribed (stamped): TIFFANY STUDIOS NEW YORK 1596.
First introduced in 1899, there were over 125 designs for Tiffany leaded glass lampshades available by 1906. The Haworth example, though relatively plain, was still a luxury product and would have cost about $30. One-off shades made for specially commissioned interiors might cost as much as $750. Clara Driscoll's recently-discovered correspondence reveals that she was responsible for many Tiffany lampshade designs and produced them with the help of over 60 women at Tiffany Studios. See *A New Light on Tiffany-Clara Driscoll and the Tiffany Girls* by Eidelberg et al.
Bought in 1983 with a grant from the V&A Purchase Grant Fund, public donations and a gift from Barbara Bagge and Sheila Beardmore in memory of their father Alderman William Brotherton JP, (1894-1982).
32

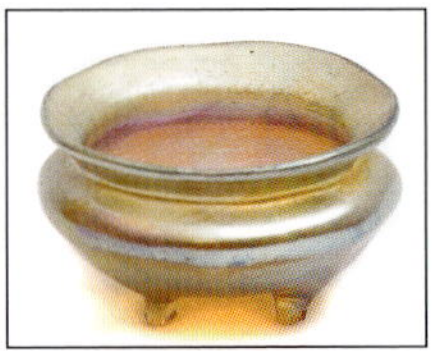

82 Salt Cellar

Iridescent gold glass, press-moulded, with irregular rim, eight sides and four 'feet'. 4.5 cm.
Salt cellars were available in this 'Witches' Cauldron' design amongst others. Thousands were produced and sold in velvet-lined canteens of every size.
Inscribed: L. C. T.
Given by Mrs Elsie Bottomley of Bingley, Yorkshire, in 1992.
35

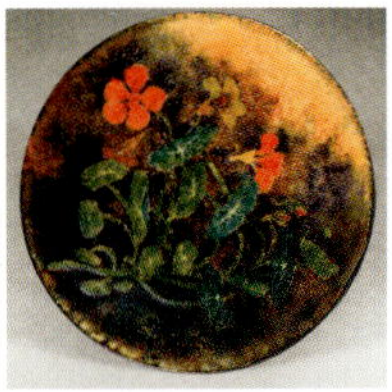

83 Enamelled Plaque

Circular copper plaque with floral polychrome decoration of Nasturtium flowers and leaves. 31 cm.
Inscribed (stamped): 9945 J
36

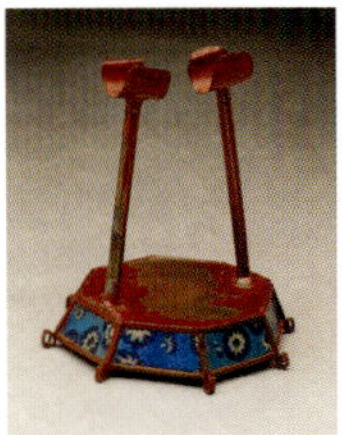

84 Pen Rest

Painted bronze, in octagonal form, with eight tiny 'feet' and decorated with eight blue *millefiori* glass panels. 12 cm.
Possibly from the 'Chinese' desk set range.
Inscribed on base: LCT
37

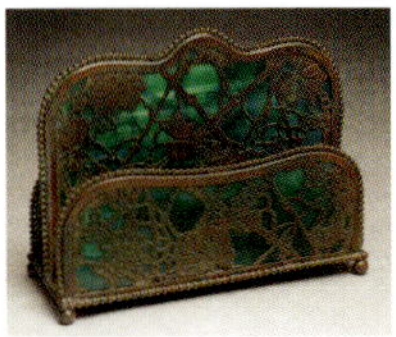

85 Small Paper Rack

Marbleised glass and bronze, with four ball 'feet'. 10.5 x 17 x 5 cm.
From the 'Etched Metal and Glass' desk set range in Pine-needle design, illustrated in Tiffany Studios' 1920 catalogue.
Inscribed (stamped): TIFFANY STUDIOS/ NEW YORK
38

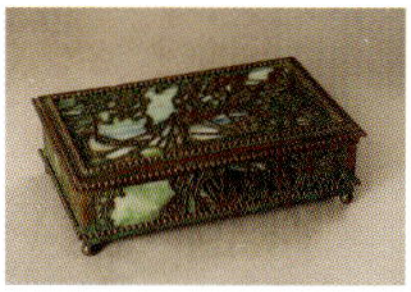

86 Stamp or Uitility Box

Marbleised glass and bronze, with four ball 'feet'. 13 x 16.5 x 7 cm.
From the 'Etched Metal and Glass' desk set range in Grapevine design, illustrated in Tiffany Studios' 1920 catalogue.
Inscribed (by hand): SK3017; (stamped): TIFFANY STUDIOS/ NEW YORK
The Box could only be bought with eight further items, the minimum for a desk set, including the small paper rack, blotter ends, ink stand and pen tray.
39

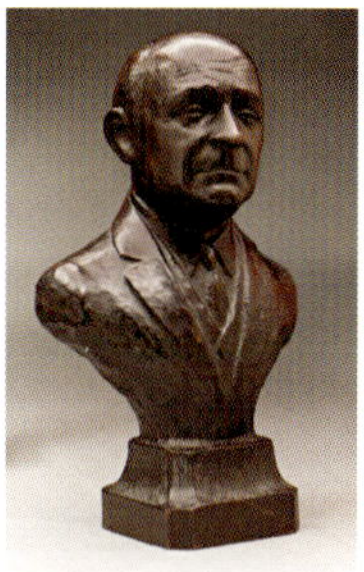

87 Portrait Bust of Joseph Briggs

Bronze. 32 cm.
Probably made by a Tiffany Studios artist when Joseph Briggs became Managing Director in 1919. The terracotta model for this bust was with Lillian Nassau Gallery, New York in October, 1998.
Unsigned; stamped, (lower left, back): TIFFANY S..DIOS/NEW ...K.
Given by Neil and Janet Harrington of Florida, USA, 1998.
40

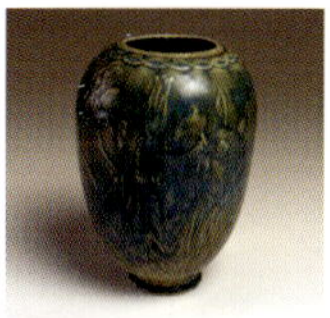

88 Cast Earthenware Vase

Ovoid form with celadon glaze, decorated with Arum Lilies. 15 cm.
Inscribed: P1224 L.C.Tiffany-Favrile Pottery
With original green/gold LCT label.
41

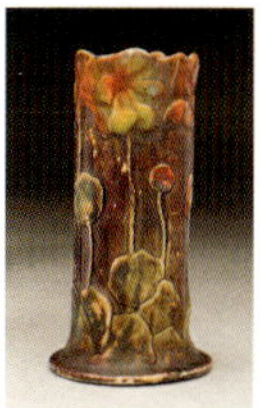

89 Cast Earthenware Vase

With red/brown glazes, decorated with Nasturtiums. 18 cm.
Inscribed: P1312/ L.C.T (monogram) Favrile/Pottery
With original green/gold LCT label and original $150 price label.
42

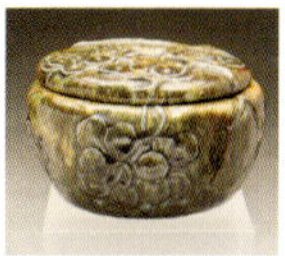

90 Cast Earthenware Bowl with Lid

In green/brown glazes, decorated with Honesty. 8 x12 cm.
Inscribed: P.1416 LCT (monogram)
43

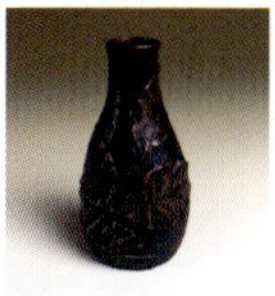

91 Cast Earthenware Vase

Cased with gold-lustred bronze and decorated with large leaves. 15 cm.
Inscribed: BP260 /L.C.Tiffany. Favrile /Bronze Pottery./LCT (monogram)
Exhibited: Hamburg, 1999 (no. 233).
44

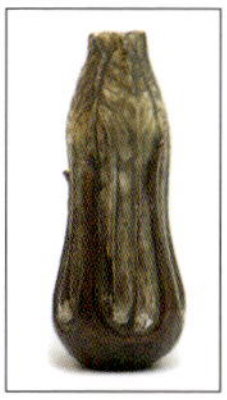

92 Cast Earthenware Vase

In the form of a closed dandelion flower, silvered and cradled in a bronze mount. 25 cm.
Inscribed on base: J Briggs/1921
Exhibited: Hamburg, 1999 (no. 234).
45

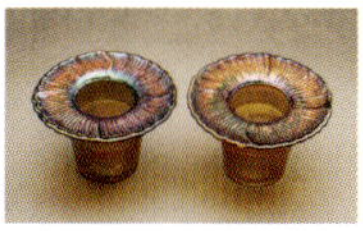

93 Pair of Candle Holders

Press-moulded iridescent glass. 4.5 cm x 6.5 cm.
Both inscribed: L.C.T.Favrile
Given by Peter T. Swan of New South Wales, Australia, 2009.
144

Glass Tiles, Jewels and Panels

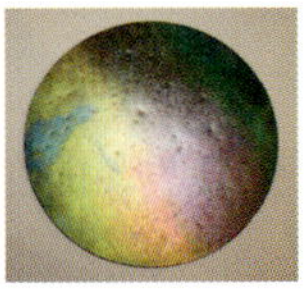

94 Circular Panel

Showing iridescent rainbow-colour effects, as developed by Tiffany for stained glass windows in the 1880s and for blown glass in 1895. Diameter 16.5 cm.

1

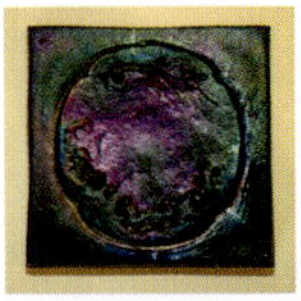

95 Iridescent purple/blue Tile

In two layers with Chinese-style design. 10 x 10 cm.

2

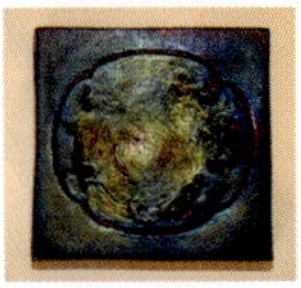

96 Iridescent green/blue Tile

In two layers with Chinese-style design. Press identical to cat. no. 95. 10 x 10 cm.
Tiles like these were used in early Tiffany interiors, like the fireplace surround in the Armory of 1879.

3

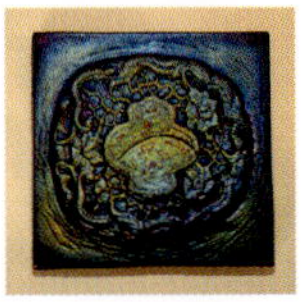

97 Iridescent green/blue Tile

In two layers with a design of leaves and berries. 10 x 10 cm.

4

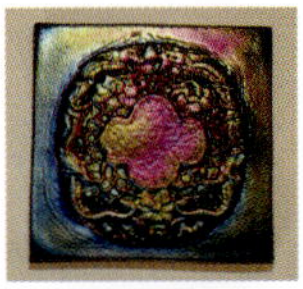

98 Iridescent purple/gold/blue Tile

In two layers with a design of leaves and berries. Press identical to cat. no. 97. 10 x 10 cm.

5

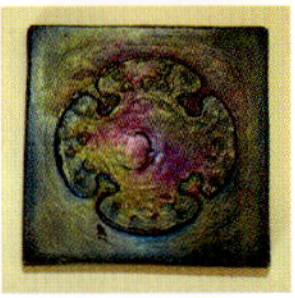

99 Iridescent purple/gold/blue Tile

In two layers with Japanese-style design. 10 x 10 cm.

6

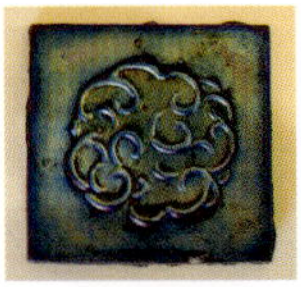

100 Iridescent blue Tile

In two layers with 'five-petalled rosette' design and pink/silver effects. 10 x 10 cm.

7

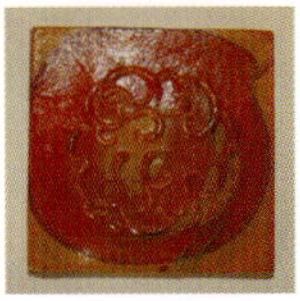

101 Orange /red Tile

With red circular brush line over 'five-petalled rosette' design. Press identical to cat. no. 100. 10 x 10 cm.

8

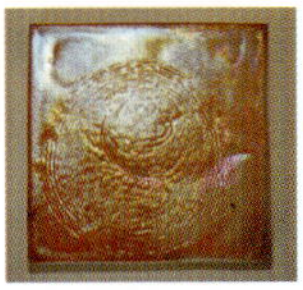

102 Iridescent orange Tile

With subtle surface undulation and circular patterning. The reverse has four 'stars' to assist keying-in to a vertical surface. 10 x 10 cm.

9

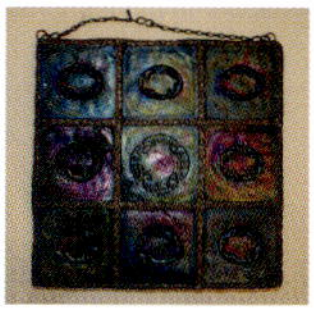

103 Leaded Sampler of nine iridescent blue Tiles, with hanging chain

Eight tiles showing Dragon design, the ninth central tile
showing Chinese-style design. 31.5 x 31.5 cm. (chain 32 cm).
10

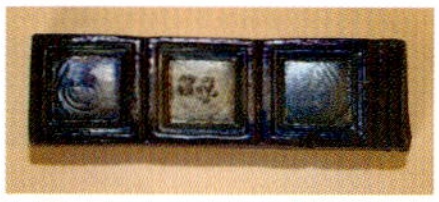

104 Iridescent blue edging Tile

With three one-inch squares, water ripples and rounded finish to make an edge. 11 x 3 cm.
11

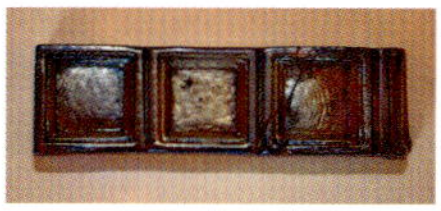

105 Iridescent yellow edging Tile

With three one-inch squares, water ripples and rounded finish to make an edge. 11 x 3 cm.
12

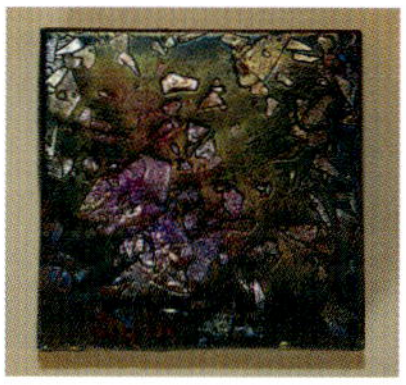

106 Iridescent green Confetti Tile

In two layers, the lower of opalescent glass, the upper with angular fragments of glass scattered on to its surface. This effect increased colour density and the play of light in stained glass windows. Similar tiles were used in the Loggia of Laurelton Hall, Tiffany's Long Island home.
Reverse has four 'stars' for keying-in. 7.4 x 7.4 cm.
13

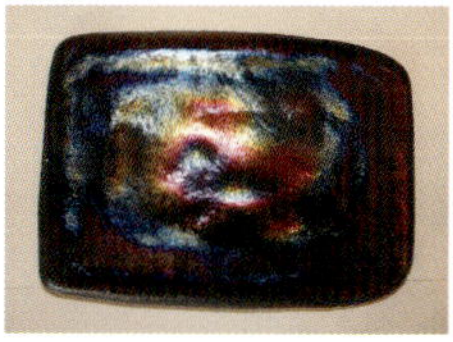

107 Iridescent blue Turtleback Tile

With rainbow-colour effects, enhanced by the irregular organic form of the tile. Made by dropping molten glass in to a mould; the glass left to find its own level. 19.5 x 14 cm.
Tiffany used Turtlebacks like this to edge the pool in the *Garden Landscape and Fountain* dated 1905-1915, Metropolitan Museum of Art, New York.
14

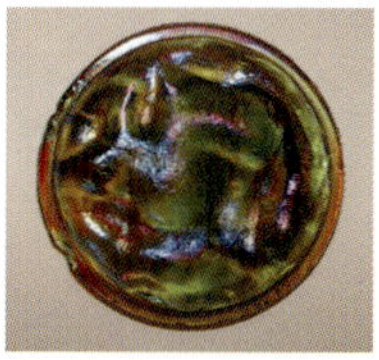

108 Iridescent green Jewel

Circular format with transparent finish, wave forms and indented edge. Diameter 7 cm.
Exhibited: Hamburg, 1999 (no. 11e).
[inv.1999.33.48] 15

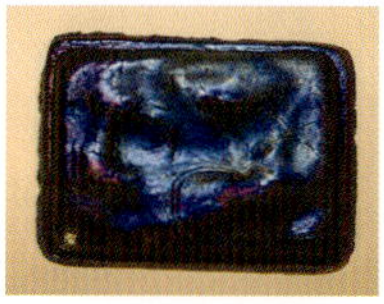

109 Iridescent blue Jewel

Oblong format with matt finish, wave forms and indented edge. 7 x 5.5 cm.
Exhibited: Hamburg, 1999 (no. 11g).
[inv.1999.33.50] 16

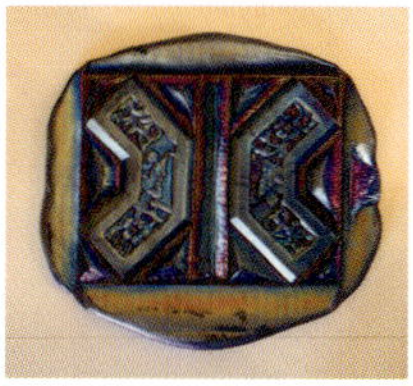

110 Untrimmed iridescent blue Tile

Decorated with two 'V'shapes containing floral patterns. The press combines the hand-made quality of the edges of the 'V' with mechanical quality in the floral pattern. The untrimmed residue of glass around the tile shows its fluidity before cooling. 13 x 14 cm.
17

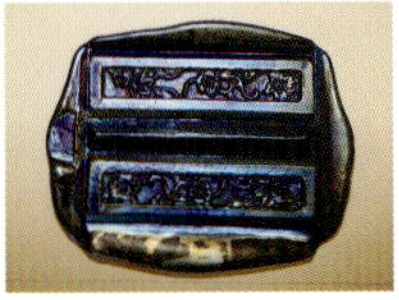

111 Untrimmed iridescent blue Tile

The design has both hand-made and mechanical qualities as in cat. no. 110. This tile also shows the untrimmed residue of the press-moulding process. 10 x 12.5 cm.
18

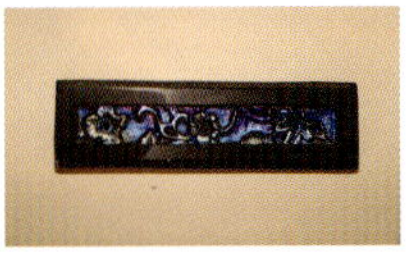

112 Iridescent blue Tile

Press identical to cat. no. 111 but cut from the mould and polished. 8.5 x 2.3 cm.
19

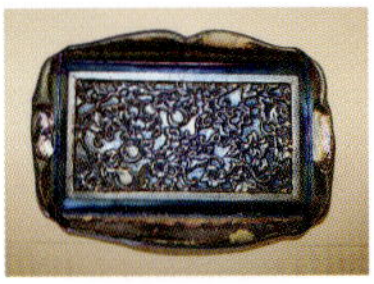

113 Untrimmed iridescent blue Tile

With floral pattern used in cat. no. 110 to 112, set in to oblong. 13 x18 cm.
21

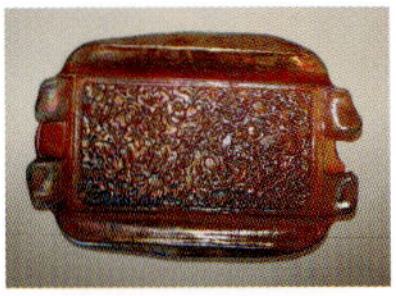

114 Untrimmed iridescent yellow Tile

Floral pattern, a variation of that used in cat. nos. 110 to 113, set in to oblong. 14.5 x 21.5 cm.
22

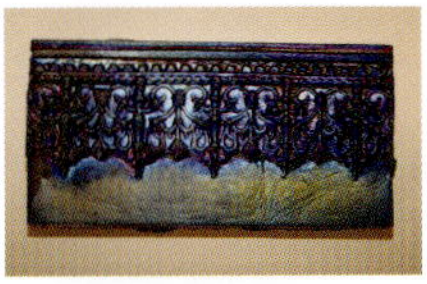

115 Iridescent blue Tile

Decorated with lace pattern. 7 x 13.5 cm.
20

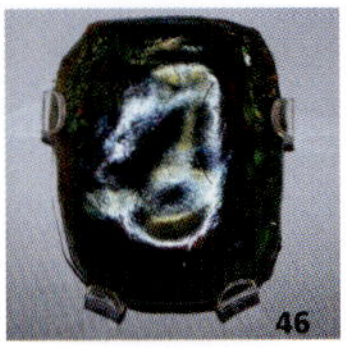

116 Iridescent green Turtleback tile

Oblong format with semi-transparent finish. Made by dropping molten glass in to a mould; the glass left to find its own level. 12 x 14 cm.
46

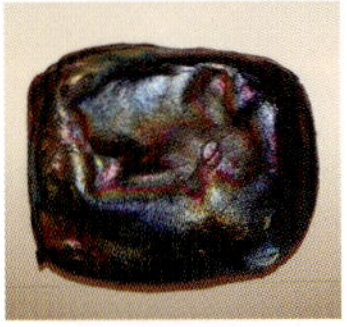

117 Iridescent blue Turtleback tile

Oblong format with opaque finish. Made as cat. no. 116, possibly in the same mould. 12 x 14 cm.
47

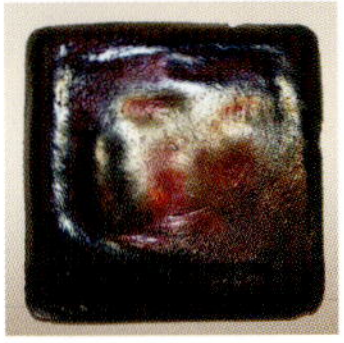

118 Iridescent green Turtleback tile

Made as above (cat. no. 117) but using a square mould. 13.5 x 13.5 cm.
48

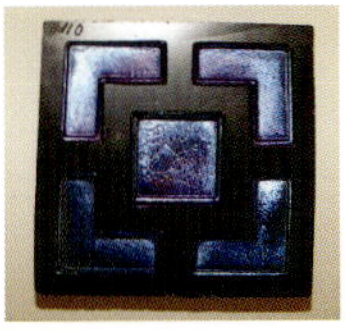

119 Iridescent blue Tile

With square design in relief. 10 x 10 cm.
Tile similar to those used in a fireplace in the New Jersey residence of Mrs Louis G Kaufman around 1911-1915 and by Joseph Briggs for the fireplace at his home 'Wood Ridge' in New Jersey.
Marked #110 on face, top left-hand side and on top edge.
49

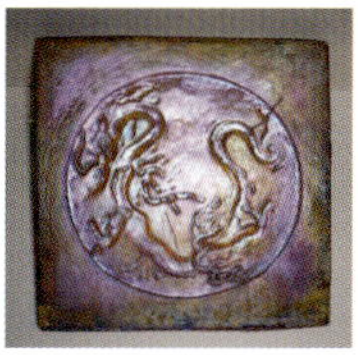

120 Iridescent yellow Tile

With double dragon motif, the type used by Tiffany in the Entrance Hall of Laurelton Hall, his Long Island home. 10 x 10 cm.
71

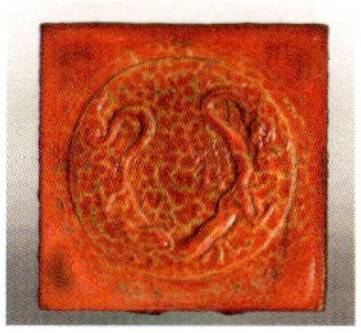

121 Red Tile

With double dragon motif, represented as a positive image of cat. no. 120 above and ball 'feet' set in to reverse for keying-in. 10 x 10 cm.
[inv.1999.33.84] 72

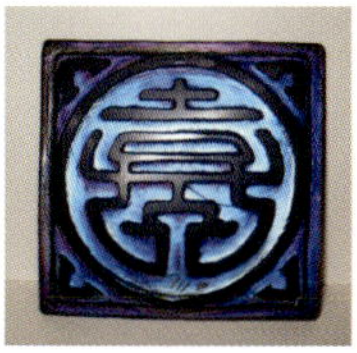

122 Lustred blue Tile

Decorated with pseudo-Chinese script, marked:# 111. This tile and cat. nos. 120 and 121 date from pre-1892 when Tiffany established his own glass works at Corona, Long Island. 9 x 9 cm.
73

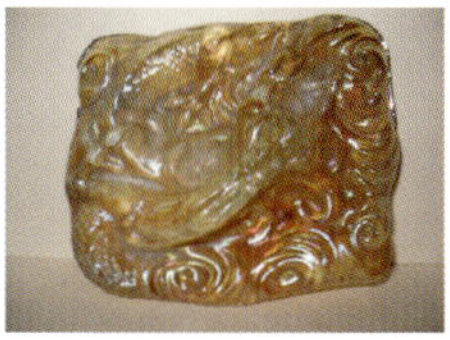

123 Iridescent yellow Tile

In very high relief, decorated with sea creature amongst water swirls. Probably made for a specific space in a decorative scheme. 14 x 12 cm.
Exhibited: Hamburg, 1999 (no. 11d).
[inv. 1999.33.47] 74

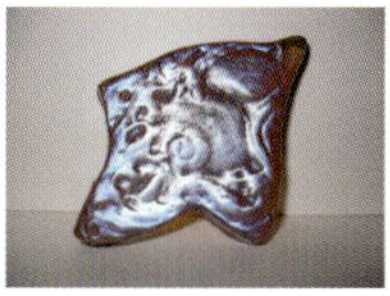

124 Iridescent green Jewel

With irregular, four-sided format and marine-inspired forms. 8 x 10 cm.
Exhibited: Hamburg, 1999 (no. 11f).
[inv. 1999.33.49] 75

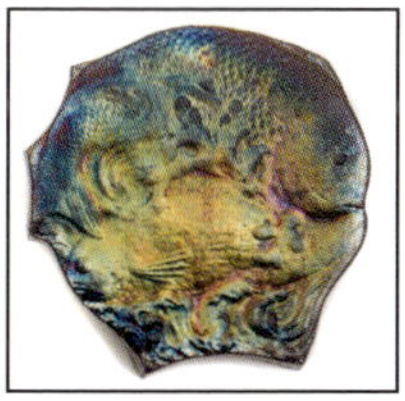

125 Iridescent blue Tile

Irregular press-moulded shape decorated with two entwined fish amongst seaweed and waves. Probably made for a specific space in a decorative scheme. 16 cm.
Exhibited: Hamburg, 1999 (no. 11b).
[inv.1999.33.45] 76

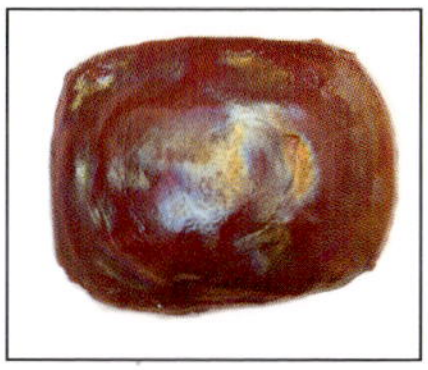

126 Iridescent red Turtleback Tile

Turtleback tiles in red are rare owing to the cost of making red glass. 12 x 15 cm.
Exhibited Hamburg, 1999 (no. 11c).
[inv.1999.33.46] 77

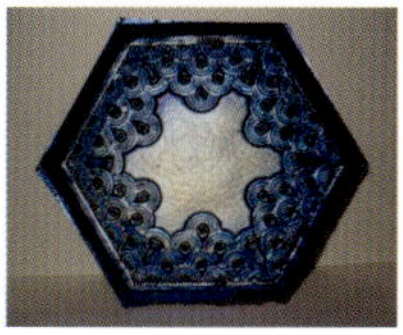

127 Iridescent blue Tile

Hexagonal Chinese-inspired tile, with wave pattern incorporating peacock feather 'eyes'. 13 x 15 cm.
Exhibited Hamburg, 1999 (no. 11a).
[inv.1999.33.44] 78

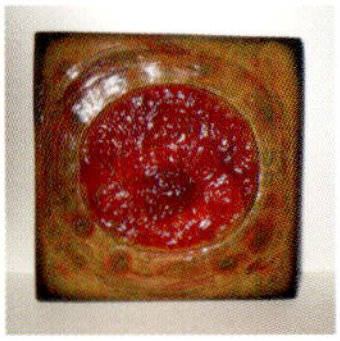

128 Orange Tile

With central red fire motif and darkened edges. 10 x 10 cm.
79

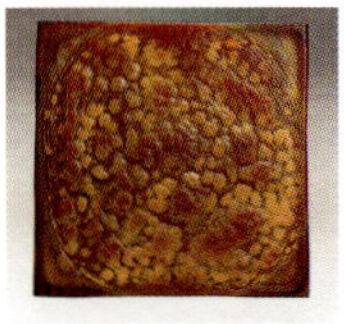

129 Speckled Tile

With red and orange circular brushline decoration. 10 x 10 cm.
Reverse has squares for keying-in.
Pressed along rim: PAT APPLIED FOR
[inv.1999.33.89] 88

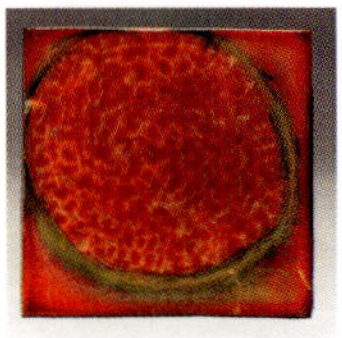

130 Red Tile

With green circlular brushline decoration. 10 x 10 cm.
Reverse has 'stars' for keying-in
Pressed along rim: PATENT APPLIED FOR
89

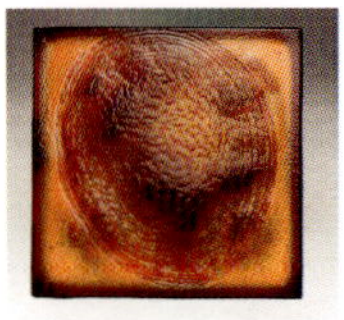

131 Orange Tile

With red circular brushline decoration. 10 x 10 cm.
Reverse has 'stars' for keying-in.
Pressed along rim: PATENT APPLIED FOR
[inv.1999.33.88] 90

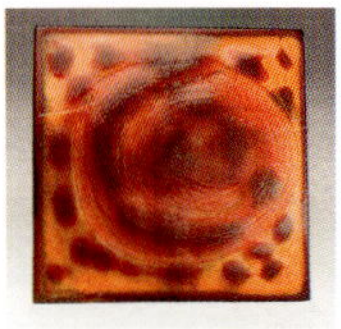

132 Large orange Tile

With red and orange speckled and circular brushline decoration. 15.2 x 15.2 cm.
Reverse has 'stars' for keying-in.
Pressed along rim: PATENT APPLIED FOR
91

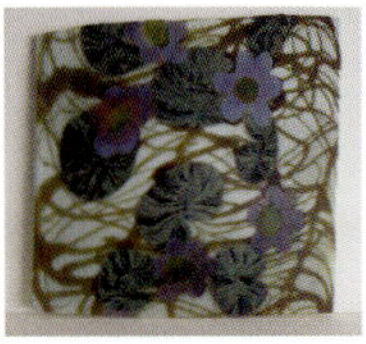

133 Opalescent white *millefiori* Panel

Decorated with pond weed, fronds, Lily-pads and blue and mauve blossoms. 24 cm.
Panel similar to one sold at Christies, New York, 12/5/2003, formerly in the collection of the Museum of Modern Art, New York.
100

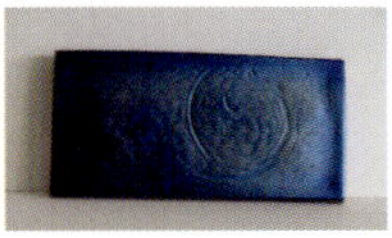

134 Iridescent blue Tile

Rectangular with matt finish and circular forms. 10 x 5 cm.
Reverse has two 'stars' for keying-in.
101

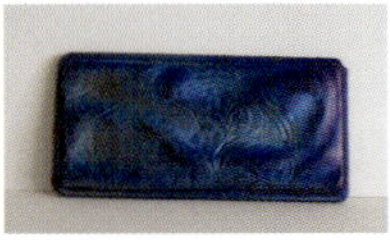

135 Iridescent blue Tile

Rectangular with matt finish and wavy surface and indented around edge. 9.8 x 5 cm.
Pressed on reverse: OBLONG.
102

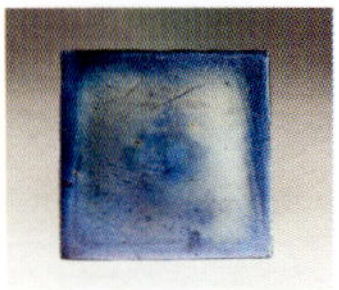

136 Iridescent blue Tile

Matt finish with subtle surface forms. 5 x 5 cm.
Reverse has 'star' for keying-in.
103

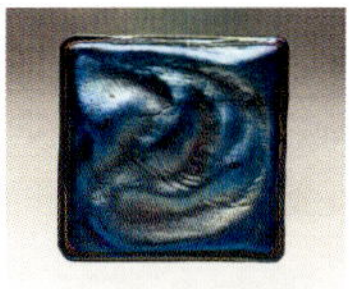

137 Iridescent blue Tile

With green/purple colour effects and rippled surface. 6.3 x 6.3 cm.
104

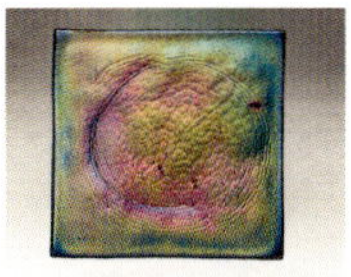

138 Iridescent blue Tile

Matt blue tile in two layers, with subtle surface patterning. 10 x 10 cm.
Reverse has four 'stars' for keying-in.
Pressed on reverse: PATENT APPLIED FOR.
105

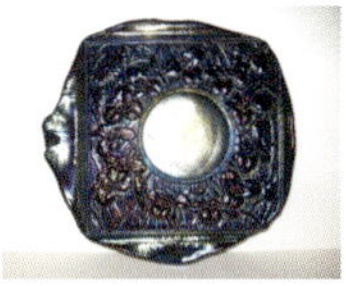

139 Untrimmed iridescent blue Panel

Square format with circle surrounded with Orchids, two corners curved to fit a specific place. The residue of glass around the tile shows its fluidity before cooling. 16 cm.
131

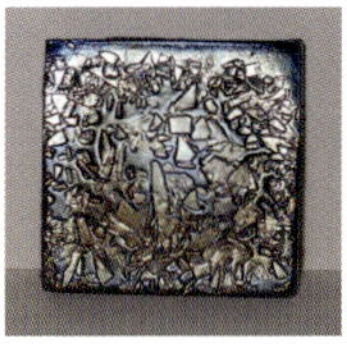

140 Iridescent blue Confetti Tile

Small version of cat. no. 106, with angular fragments across surface. 6 x 6 cm.
132

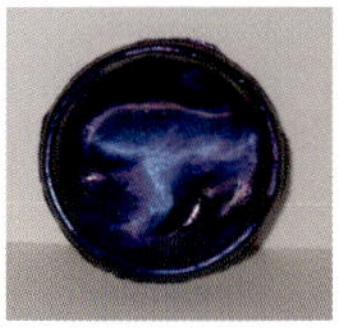

141 Iridescent blue Jewel

Circular format with matt finish and water ripples. Diameter 6 cm.
Exhibited Hamburg, 1999 (no. 11h).
[inv.1999.33.51]
133

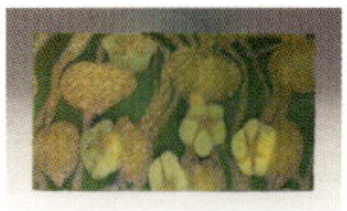

142 Iridescent green *millefiori* Sample

Decorated with lilac/green Lily-pads. 8 x 14 cm.
139

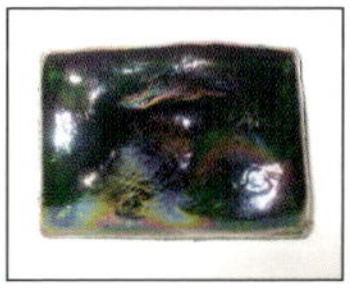

143 Iridescent blue Jewel

Oblong, decorated with wavy undulations. 8 x 6 cm.
Exhibited: Hamburg, 1999 (no. 11i).
[inv.1999.33.52]
140

Haworth Archive

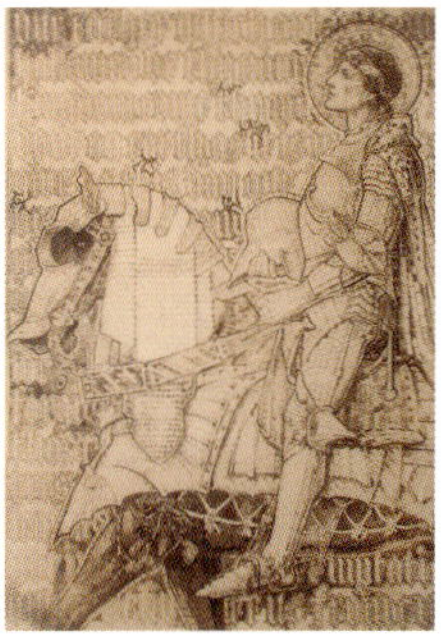

144 St George and the Dragon

Sepia photograph of pen and ink drawing, showing the partial schematisation of the preliminary sketch (cat. no. 73) to show how glass tesserae should be cut to achieve the desired design. Cat. no. 74 shows the realisation of the top left-hand corner of the proposed memorial.
Artist unknown. 22 x 16 cm.
Inscribed on reverse in pencil:17799-cartoon (and) 134.

Acknowledgements

This book about the Haworth's Tiffany glass collection has been produced through the generous bequest of the late Stephen Moore of Altham in Accrington. Hyndburn Borough Council and Jennifer Rennie would like to thank his family for their help with the arrangements.

We would also like to thank Ann Bukantas, Head of Fine Art, National Museums Liverpool (NML) for her most generous editorial support at all stages during the preparation of the text and Karen Miller, Publications Manager NML, for suggestions on all aspects of production. Penny Johnson, Curator of the Government Art Collection, has given invaluable advice on the publication and Andrew Baldwin, Helen Barrett, Susan Dodd, David Edmunds and Christopher Sheldon have helped with research, proof-reading and photography. Finally, thank you to Haworth Art Gallery Staff and to Eric Knowles for his continued, enthusiastic support for the Haworth and its extraordinary Tiffany glass collection.

Design

Val Evans

Photography Credits

Tiffany collection catalogue numbers. All others as stated.

Susan Dodd: 120, 122 to 124, 127, 128, 133, 139-141, 143.

Andrew Ford: 2, 3, 4, 7, 19, 30, 44, 47, 50, 52, 54, 72, 75, 80, 82, 92, 125, 126. Also *Arts and Crafts motifs* on pages 7, 15 and 23.

Richard Lewis: 6, 8, 10, 12, 13, 16, 18, 20, 22, 24-26, 28, 31-41, 43, 45, 46, 48, 49, 51, 53, 55, 57-59, 61, 62, 64, 73, 76, 78, 79, 83-87, 89, 90, 93, 121, 129-132, 136-138, 142.

Barry Stacey: 1, 5, 9, 11, 14, 15, 17, 21, 23, 27, 29, 42, 48a, 56, 60, 66, 67, 74, 77, 81, 88, 91, 144. Also *Selection of Tiles and Jewels,* page 15 and Base of *Millefiore Paperweight Vase,* opposite page.

Christopher Sheldon: 94 to 119.

F Westall: *The Haworth's Music Room,* page 9.

Further Reading

Crouch, Edith. *The Mosaics of Louis Comfort Tiffany,* Schiller, USA, 2009

Eidelberg, Martin, Gray, Nina and Hofer, Margaret. *A New Light on Tiffany-Clara Driscoll and the Tiffany Girls,* New York Historical Society, exhibition catalogue, 2007

Eidelberg, Martin. *Tiffany Favrile Glass and the Quest of Beauty,* New York, Lillian Nassau Gallery, 2007

Frelinghuysen, Alice Cooney. *Louis Comfort Tiffany at the Metropolitan Museum,* Reprint of the Metropolitan Museum of Art Bulletin, New York, 1998

Johnson, Marilynn et al. *Louis Comfort Tiffany-Artist for the Ages,* catalogue for the exhibition in Seattle, Toledo, Dallas and Pittsburg, USA, 2005

Koch, Robert. *Louis C. Tiffany: The Collected Works of Robert Koch,* Schiller, USA, 2001

Pepall, Rosalind et al. *Tiffany Glass - A Passion for Colour,* catalogue for the exhibition in Paris, Montreal and Richmond, USA, 2009

Potter, Norman and Jackson, Douglas. *Tiffany,* London, 1988

Base of **Millefiore Paperweight Vase**
cat. no. 48